Polyamory, Monogamy, and American Dreams is a much needed book which radically rethinks the ways in which relationships are understood, represented, and lived in US culture. Taking a poly gaze to everything from mainstream movies to hook-up research, the author points out the skewed perspectives that take a monogamous white, western, norm as their starting point. In times of austerity and neofacism this book offers much-needed alternative perspectives on how we might transform our ways of living and relating if we deploy a poly gaze.

Dr. Meg-John Barker, author of Rewriting the Rules,
Understanding Non-Monogamies, *and* Life Isn't Binary

In *Polyamory, Monogamy, and American Dreams*, Mimi Schippers trains a polyqueer gaze on cultural narratives from *Camelot* to *Grace and Frankie*, unearthing the possibility for connections of care, mutuality, belonging, and intimacy beyond ties of marriage or blood. She teaches us how to identify mononormativity embedded in the stories we tell—and to see the way that it perpetuates inequalities. This courageous, creative, compassionate book provides new ways to think about the culture we consume and the lives we create.

Elizabeth A. Armstrong, Professor of Sociology and Organizational Studies,
University of Michigan

Polyamory, Monogamy, and American Dreams offers an urgent interruption of our understanding of sex and love in modern times. From critiquing the sexual styles of American exceptionalism to imploding notions of the good life, through this book's 'poly gaze' you'll never see the world the same again.

Hannah McCann, Lecturer in Cultural Studies, University of Melbourne

Arguably the most revolutionary idea to hit gender and sexuality studies in a decade, the poly gaze is more than a lens on polyamory. It's a prism that reveals how mononormativity inflects all axes of oppression and an essential tool for social justice. Schippers paves an inspiring path toward a more poly politics, one that binds us together instead of holds us apart.

Lisa Wade, Associate Professor of Sociology, Occidental College and author of
American Hookup: The New Culture of Sex on Campus

POLYAMORY, MONOGAMY, AND AMERICAN DREAMS

This book introduces "the poly gaze" as a cultural tool to examine how representations of polyamory and poly lives reflect or challenge cultural hegemonies of race, class, gender, and nation.

What role does monogamy play in American Identity, the American dream, and U.S. exceptionalism? How do the stories we tell about intimate relationships do cultural and ideological work to maintain and legitimize social inequalities along the lines of race, ethnicity, nation, religion, class, gender, and sexuality? How might the introduction of polyamory or consensually non-monogamous relationships in the stories we tell about intimacy confound, disrupt, or shift the meaning of what constitutes a good, American life? These are the questions that Mimi Schippers focuses on in this original and engaging study. As she develops the *poly gaze*, Schippers argues for a sociologically informed and cultivated lens with which anyone, regardless of their experiences with polyamory or consensual non-monogamy, can read culture, media images, and texts against hegemony.

This will be a key text for researchers and students in Gender Studies, Queer Studies, Cultural Studies, Critical Race Studies, Media Studies, American Studies, and Sociology. This book is accessible and indispensable reading for undergraduate students and postgraduates wanting to gain greater understanding of debates around the key concept of heteronormativity.

Mimi Schippers received her PhD in Sociology from the University of Wisconsin-Madison and is Professor of Sociology and Gender and Sexuality Studies at Tulane University. Her research focuses on masculinities, femininities, and the intersections of gender, race, and sexuality in everyday interactions, relationships, and subcultures. She is author of *Beyond Monogamy: Polyamory and the Future of Polyqueer Sexualities* and *Rockin' Out of the Box: Gender Maneuvering in Alternative Hard Rock*.

FEMINISM AND FEMALE SEXUALITY

POLYAMORY, MONOGAMY, AND AMERICAN DREAMS

The Stories We Tell about Poly Lives and the Cultural Production of Inequality

Mimi Schippers

Routledge
Taylor & Francis Group

LONDON AND NEW YORK

First published 2020
by Routledge
2 Park Square, Milton Park, Abingdon, Oxon OX14 4RN

and by Routledge
52 Vanderbilt Avenue, New York, NY 10017

Routledge is an imprint of the Taylor & Francis Group, an informa business

British Library Cataloguing in Publication Data
A catalogue record for this book is available from the British Library

Library of Congress Cataloging-in-Publication Data
Names: Schippers, Mimi, 1964- author.
Title: Polyamory, monogamy, and American dreams : the stories we tell about
  poly lives and the cultural production of inequality / Mimi Schippers.
Description: Milton Park, Abingdon, Oxon ; New York, NY : Routledge, 2020.
  | Includes bibliographical references and index.
Identifiers: LCCN 2019028301 (print) | LCCN 2019028302 (ebook) | ISBN
  9781138895034 (paperback) | ISBN 9781138895010 (hardback) | ISBN
  9781315179698 (ebook) | ISBN 9781351717120 (adobe pdf) | ISBN
  9781351717113 (epub) | ISBN 9781351717106 (mobi)
Subjects: LCSH: Non-monogamous relationships–United States. | Interpersonal
  relations–United States. | Equality–United States.
Classification: LCC HQ980.5 .S35 2020 (print) | LCC HQ980.5 (ebook) |
  DDC 306.84/23–dc23
LC record available at https://lccn.loc.gov/2019028301
LC ebook record available at https://lccn.loc.gov/2019028302

ISBN: 978-1-138-89501-0 (hbk)
ISBN: 978-1-138-89503-4 (pbk)
ISBN: 978-1-315-17969-8 (ebk)

Typeset in Bembo
by Taylor & Francis Books

CONTENTS

FIGURES

PREFACE

One of my favorite films is the 1967 musical drama *Camelot* (Logan 1967). When I first saw it at the age of 14, I was enthralled with the costumes, the music, and the mythical story of King Arthur, Guinevere, and Lancelot. Though the film was quite dated by the time I encountered it on a VHS tape my mother acquired, I still lost myself in the love story between Arthur, the reluctant King of England, Guinevere the seductive Queen, and the handsome French knight, Lancelot. It is, above all else, a romantic narrative about love and betrayal, and one might conclude that my love of this film was nothing more than just another example of an adolescent girl's fascination with tales of heterosexual romance. Although I am certain romance was part of it, in retrospect, I believe there was something more that drew me in.

The film begins with Arthur and Guinevere meeting in the mythical forests outside of the Kingdom of Camelot. They are about to embark on an arranged marriage, and though Guinevere is at first quite reluctant, Arthur convinces her that Camelot is the place for "happily ever after-ing." Deeply and blissfully in love, adored across their kingdom, and working together to set up a new set of fair and just laws embodied by the knights of the round table, Arthur and Guinevere appear to have indeed grasped happily-ever-after. That is, until Lancelot, the handsome, skillful, and insufferably self-righteous French knight, rides into the story, quite literally, on his white stallion.

Arthur and Guinevere have different and opposing first impressions of Lancelot. Arthur is impressed with Lancelot's commitment to the physical and moral ideals of knighthood, so he takes Lancelot under his wing as his "right hand" and best friend. Unlike Arthur, Guinevere is initially annoyed by Lancelot's self-professed purity and perfection, and she is jealous of the attention he gets from her husband. To deflate Lancelot's ego and reveal his claims of perfection as narcissistic fantasy, she seductively cajoles three other knights to challenge him to a joust. Lancelot bests each of the three knights in succession—his skills so unworldly that, when he fatally wounds his last opponent with a mighty blow, Lancelot brings him back to life. Guinevere watches Lancelot strip the dead knight of his armor, massage his wounded, naked chest, and place his lips to the other knight's and whisper "Live-Live-Live." When, through sheer will, Lancelot brings his opponent back from the dead, Guinevere, too, becomes quite smitten with the young Frenchman.

Both Arthur and Guinevere love Lancelot in their own way, but it is Guinevere who, after a montage of shy and seductive glances, consummates her love for Lancelot by, late one night, entering his chambers and falling into his bed. As Arthur comes to realize that Guinevere and Lancelot are lovers, he is torn between their shared commitment to Camelot and the roundtable on the one hand, and the betrayal of infidelity on the other.

Half-way through the film, Arthur's dilemma is in need of resolution, and if other stories about love triangles are any indication, we might expect him to use his power as the king to force Lancelot out of the picture and claim Guinevere as his own or take retribution on both of them. We might also expect that Lancelot will use whatever he has at his disposal—namely his good looks and fighting skills—to eliminate Arthur and take sole possession of Guinevere. And we would not be at all surprised if Guinevere, the prized object of both men's affections, sat back and let the best man win.

The love triangle in *Camelot*, however, is not like most others. Instead of fighting Lancelot or hauling both Lancelot and Guinevere into the public square and punishing them for their treason to crown and country, Arthur comes to accept their affair and protects them from exposure. In fact, it is Arthur who, in an over-the-top, melodramatic soliloquy, explicitly articulates this rather unconventional resolution to erotic triangulation.

> Proposition: If I could choose, from every woman who breathes on this earth…every detail and feature to the smallest strand of hair—they would all be Jenny's.
>
> Proposition: If I could choose from every man who breathes on this earth, a man for my brother and a man for my son, a man for my friend, they would all be Lance. Yes, I love them. I Love them, and they answer me with pain and torment. Be it sin or not sin, they betray me in their hearts, and that's far sin enough. I see it in their eyes and feel it when they speak, and they must pay for it and be punished…
>
> Proposition: I'm a king, not a man. And a very civilized king. Could it possibly be civilized to destroy the thing I love? Could it possibly be civilized to love myself above all? What about their pain? And their torment? Did they ask for this calamity? Can passion be selected? Is there any doubt of their devotion to me? To our table…This is the time of King Arthur, and violence is not strength and compassion is not weakness. We are civilized! Resolved: We shall live through this together.

Though clearly betrayed and initially wanting vengeance, Arthur accepts the adulterous relationship between Lancelot and Guinevere and does so because they all love each other and because he is a "civilized" king, not a vengeful man. "Violence is not strength and compassion is not weakness," he says. And so the three of them "shall live through this together."

King Arthur offers an interesting alternative to the kinds of men or kings we usually see in narrative film—those who, in the affairs of the state or the heart, deploy violence to exact vengeance to protect or reclaim power and resources, including sole possession of women. Contrary to what we might expect, the narrative resolution to erotic triangulation in *Camelot* is not winner-takes-all. Instead, Arthur acknowledges the mutual love among all three and, by doing so, solves his dilemma by moving forward together.

The love triangle between Arthur, Guinevere, and Lancelot, as narrated in this film, offers a glimpse of something akin to what is now called in contemporary parlance, *polyamory*. What I mean is that, although written and produced long before the word "polyamory" was coined by Morning Glory Zell-Ravenheart in 1999, the film depicts an emotionally intimate and on-going relationship between three rather than two adults, and everybody is aware of and (eventually) consents to the arrangement—the very definition of polyamory.

Certainly the love triangle in *Camelot* is not *really* polyamory if we take seriously the cultural specificity of polyamory as an emergent sexual subculture in contemporary, mostly Western, societies. After all, neither the word nor any intelligible articulation of its meaning existed when the screenplay was written and the film made. For this reason it would be socio-historically inaccurate to refer to *Camelot* as a film *about* polyamory.[1] Although we cannot call *Camelot* a film about polyamory, I wish to argue that it is *poly narrative* where a multi-adult relationship (in this case three adults—Arthur, Guinevere, and Lancelot) is a central feature of character development and plot structure and displaces the monogamous couple as narrative resolution.

Arthur's soliloquy clearly establishes a solution to his predicament that looks a lot more poly (we'll live through this together as three) than mono (re-establishment of monogamy). Also, and more central to my purposes in this book, by rejecting the trope of a winner-take-all, this film manages to sidestep not just monogamous coupling but also a portrayal of masculinity as possessive, controlling, and violent. Arthur's acceptance of Guinevere and Lancelot's relationship punctuates his compassionate, just, and "civilized" masculinity as the impetus for his new order of knights who "fight for right" rather than "for might." In other words, this poly (amorous) rather than mono(gamous) twist in the story opened a narrative path to, in a sense, *queer* their love triangle and, by doing so, establish Arthur as an extraordinarily compassionate and just man.

The film as text and narrative offers a different story about relationships, romance, erotic triangulation, and gender. Embedded within broader American discourses that define monogamous coupling as the key to happiness, the "good life," and living happily ever after, *Camelot* presents an alternative discourse. Could it be that this kind of poly rather than mono triangulation between Guinevere, Lancelot, and Arthur is precisely the reason my adolescent self loved this romance narrative more than all the others? Was the nascent, queer-desiring feminist in me hailed by a representation of the sort of polyamorous relationships and alternative masculinities I would come to desire?[2]

Of course, my interpretation of *Camelot* as a *poly narrative* is not necessarily the meaning intended by the filmmakers or an interpretation that others would take away from the film. However, it is entirely possible that, as an adolescent girl, I was hailed and drawn in by the love and romance but, at the same time, because I was an adolescent *girl* expected to be complacent and possessed by boys, I interpreted Arthur's acceptance of Lancelot into his relationship with Guinevere as something different and therefore exciting and desirable. My love of the film is not only attributable to personal taste or an adolescent love of romance narratives. Perhaps it has something also to do with the pleasure derived by *reading poly narrative against gender hegemony*.

When I say that my adolescent desire for queer relationships with boys and men who embodied alternative masculinities[3] was largely nascent, I mean that the desire for something other than heteronormativity was strong, but I didn't have a sociological understanding of gender and how it influences power dynamics in heterosexual, intimate relationships. Though I had no language for why, I knew that I was uncomfortable with being a "girl" in relationship to "straight boys." I am a cisgender woman who desired boys and men, but I had no interest in playing the complacent and feminine complement to their masculinities. I also knew that there was something about "coupling" with a straight boy that would require I act like a "straight girl" in ways I found confining and intolerable. Heteronormativity (a word I would learn much later) was not for me, but at the same time I was not a lesbian. What's a queer girl who likes boys to do?

Perhaps my nascent queer feminist self saw in *Camelot* a way to *disidentify* with being a "straight girl." In his book, *Disidentifications: Queers of Color and the Performance of Politics*, Jose Esteban Munoz (2000) suggests that queers of color resist hegemonic ideology through active disidentification with culture. Munoz writes,

> Disidentification is [a] mode of dealing with dominant ideology one that neither opts to assimilate within such a structure nor strictly opposes it; rather, disidentification is a strategy that works on and against dominant ideology. Instead of buckling under the pressures of dominant ideology (identification, assimilation) or attempting to break free of its inescapable sphere (counter-identification, utopianism), this 'working on and against' is a strategy that tries to transform a cultural logic from within, always laboring to enact permanent structural change while at the same time valuing the importance of local and everyday struggles of resistance.
>
> *(Munoz 2000: 11–12)*

For Munoz, disidentificatory practices allow queers of color to neither completely identify with the heteronormativity of "home" cultures nor completely reject them. Disidentification is the process by which one reworks identities and cultural practices so they simultaneously retain that which is edifying and pleasurable while also rejecting and jettisoning what is oppressive.

As a horny adolescent who identified as a girl and who liked boys, following heteronormative romance norms and sexual scripts meant that I must fully identify as a "straight girl" and act accordingly, especially in relationship to boys but also in relationship to other girls. Not wanting to be a "straight girl" meant that I never could really identify with heteronormative straight girls in film and television. At the same time, I felt a strong romantic and sexual desire for boys and men. We might say that, in taking pleasure in the poly relationship between Guinevere, Arthur, and Lancelot, I was able to disidentify with being a straight girl. The text and my reading of it allowed me to retain what is pleasurable about heteroromance and sex (desire for and erotic experiences with boys and men) and jettison that which is oppressive (the relationship between hegemonic masculinity and femininity).

According to Munoz (2000), "Disidentification…is a survival strategy that is employed by a minority spectator…to resist and confound socially prescriptive patterns of identification" (28). As a minority spectator of sorts (an adolescent person who identifies as a girl, desires boys and men, yet has no interest in being a girl or woman in relationship to boys and men), I found in *Camelot*'s poly narrative a way to "resist or confound socially prescriptive patterns" for identifying as and being a straight girl. The poly rather than mono narrative in *Camelot* opened up space for me to take pleasure in the heterosexual romance and identify with Guinevere while, at the same time, see that she was not an object of exchange between Arthur and Lancelot. Instead, she was partnered with both.

Camelot's poly narrative opened up a possibility for disidentification with heteronormative romance. Instead of rejecting romance narratives completely, my reading of *Camelot* is a poly interpretation and a refusal to "buckle under the pressures of dominant ideology" to be hailed as a straight girl possessed by a boy. Munoz (2000) suggests, "One possible working definition of queer that we might consider is this: queers are people who have failed to turn around to the 'Hey, you there!' interpellating call of heteronormativity" (33). Hetero-normativity tells us that heterosexual, monogamous coupling is necessary and desirable because it puts us on the path to living happily ever after. As an adolescent, I refused to turn around to the "Hey, you there!" interpellating and ubiquitous call of heterosexual monogamy that saturates American media. *Camelot* offered a *poly* interpellating call, "Hey, you there!" I turned, and I have been turning to that call ever since.

Munoz begins the introduction to *Disidentifications: Queers of Color and the Performance of Politics* with a description of Marga Gomez's performance, *Margo Gomez is Pretty, Witty, and Gay*. In the performance, Gomez describes watching David Susskind interview lesbians on his show *Open End*. Munoz writes,

> Gomez paints a romantic and tragic picture of pre-Stonewall gay reality. She invests this historical moment with allure and sexiness. The performer longs for this queer and poignant model of a lesbian identity. This longing for the life should not be read as a nostalgic wish for a lost world, but instead, as the performance goes on to indicate, as a redeployment of the past that is meant to offer a critique of the present."
>
> *(Munoz 2000: 33)*

Emphasizing a redeployment of the past to critique the present, Munoz describes his own "memory" of seeing Truman Capote on the same show when, in fact, it had aired before he was born. "I mention all of this not to set the record straight," Munoz writes, "but to gesture to the revisionary aspects of my own dis-identificatory memory of Capote's performance. Perhaps I read about Capote's comment, or I may have seen a rerun of the broadcast twelve or thirteen years later. But I do know this: my memory and subjectivity reformatted that memory, letting it work within my own internal narratives of subject formation" (Munoz 2000: 4).

Several decades after my last viewing of my mother's VHS tape and well into my own poly relationships and studies of gender, sexuality, and polyamory, I purchased a DVD version of *Camelot*. As I watched it again for the first time in many years, all of those adolescent pleasures and desires flooded my memory. As the story unfolded, I was stunned by just how poly the narrative is. Until that viewing, I had not made the connections between my feminist, queer, adolescent desires and *Camelot*'s poly narrative. My telling of those connections *now* comes from a very different subject position from anything I could have cultivated *then*.

Munoz suggests that whether or not I got it "right" doesn't matter. I can read the past, not to capture a real or accurate account of what "really" happened but, instead, in order to reconstruct the past as a method for cultivating a poly subjectivity in the present. My narrative about my adolescent self is not, then, a story of the poly me from the past; it is instead a story about how I see the world now. It is not meant to claim a core, unchanged, fixed poly self that has always existed. Instead it is to forge identifications in the present and future. My poly subjectivity, in other words, is not just a way to read texts; it is a way to reclaim and reconstruct the past *as poly* and to do so for political purposes *now*. Caroline Evans and Lorraine Gamman endorse this kind of rereading texts from the past. They write,

> even texts which have overt heterosexual narratives can come over time to be seen as queer. This is because such re-readings are not ahistorical but the product of a queer cultural moment in which images have been subject to so much renegotiation (including subcultural renegotiation) that the preferred heterosexual reading has been destabilised.
>
> *(Evans and Gamman 1995: 48)*

My re-reading of *Camelot* is a product of and embedded within my own political and sociological agenda as it takes shape in this contemporary polyqueer subcultural moment (Schippers 2016).

In this book, then, my poly standpoint or subjectivity is not grounded in a polyamorous identity, trait, or psychological structure; it is an analytic lens through which anyone can view the world, identify mononormativity and its role in perpetuating inequality, and renegotiate the mononormative preferred reading of texts from the past, present, and future. Quite simply, the purpose of this book is to 1) develop what I'm calling the poly gaze as an analytic lens, 2) invite others to consider adopting a poly rather than mono interpreting lens, and 3) by way of example, demonstrate what it can tell us about social inequality.

Before getting in to it, however, there are some people I would like to thank and acknowledge. As I wrote this book, I underwent some significant changes. Some of those changes came through conversations with others about polyamory and living a poly life. Others were because of my experiences in poly relationships, and what I see happening as polyamory becomes more mainstream in New Orleans and in the media. Other changes are due to the shifting landscape of global, national, and local politics. A lot has happened during the writing of this book, and there are specific people I would like to thank for their love, support, and ongoing work in this world.

Notes

1 It is, however, entirely possible that given the film was written and produced in the socio-historical context of "free love" in the United States during the 1960s, the film-makers might have been critical of monogamy, and that critique made its way into Arthur's soliloquy.
2 I am not suggesting that I loved the film because I was "born this way" in terms of my desire for polyamory rather than monogamous couple relationships. Although I am polyamorous as an adult, I do not believe *Camelot* hailed a core polyamorous identity or sense of self in me when I was 14 years old. Instead, I am suggesting that the film hailed a nascent and largely unarticulated desire for queer relationships and masculinities *through* poly narrative.
3 See Mimi Schippers (2002). *Rockin Out of the Box: Gender Maneuvering in Alternative Hard Rock*. New Brunswick: Rutgers University Press.

ACKNOWLEDGEMENTS

I want to thank those of you who were there when I emerged from the writing and were willing to talk shop or lose our selves in revelry. This includes especially Vicki Mayer, Lisa Wade, Red Tremmel, Danielle Hidalgo, Dana Berkowitz, and Laura McKinney. There are others who were also there for revelry including (in no special order) Jay Holtman, Peter Schippers, Laura Taylor, Colleen Margolis, Tiyi Schippers, Rachael Davis, Kate Schippers, Beth Liautaud, Vic Granata, Erica Dudas, Marnie Beilin, Mike Mossing, John Allen, Kate Rushing Mutchnik, and Joy Nix. Thank you all for your friendship and support. And thank you, Scott Brothers, for being so brilliant and supportive as we dug in the dirt and walked the dark forest together so that I could better understand my poly perspective on life.

I also wish to acknowledge and thank people who have been adopting a poly gaze (though they don't call it that) for many years and before I embarked on this humble project. This includes (in no special order) Daniel Cardosa, Joreth Innkeeper, Cunning Minx, Lusty Guy, Pepper Mint, Christian Klesse, Isa Lutine, Meg-John Barker, Elisabeth Sheff, Sina Muscarina, Serina Anderlini, Alex Iantaffi, Andrew Sparksfire, Kate Frank, Katie Klabusich, and countless other bloggers, podcasters, filmmakers, and writers. Thank you for your work and for making my job so much easier. I want to also acknowledge all of the students who are currently researching and theorizing polyamory and poly lives, including Alicia McGraw and Lital Pascar. Thank you for taking up the mantle.

I want to thank the people at Routledge, including Kitty Imbert and Alexandra McGregor, for your interest in this project and for your patience and guidance.

Finally, and always, thank you, Marc, Scott, Stevie, Ansel, and Reynard. You are my inter-species family, and I cherish your love, support, and friendship.

1

INTRODUCTION TO THE POLY GAZE

Mononormative narrative, poly narrative, and social inequality

This is a book about the stories collectively told in U.S. culture about intimate relationships, happiness, citizenship, and living a good life. Specifically, my focus is on how media representations of poly relationships, from polygamy and polyamory to sexual relationships in campus hookup cultures and sex clubs, portray non-monogamy as un-American, unsustainable, a curious anomaly, an immature phase, or, in some cases, as a viable choice or a political alternative to heteronormative monogamy. By focusing on several different kinds of texts, I hope to develop a conceptual framework for reading media with what I am calling a *poly gaze*. [1]

Poly is, for my purposes in this book, a broader term than "polyamorous." Polyamory is a very specific and contemporary label for the practice of having more than one significant, emotionally and/or sexually intimate partner. Although people have been forging non-monogamous, anti-monogamous, and plural (poly) relationships throughout history and across cultures, the word "polyamory" wasn't coined until 1999 and has become a subculture only in the last decade or so (Ritchie and Barker 2006; Sheff 2014). In the United States, Canada, the UK, and other Western European contexts, polyamory is emerging as an increasingly viable and visible relationship structure. Several books outline what polyamory is (e.g. Anapol 2010: Easton and Hardy 2009; Sheff 2014), how to pursue and maintain polyamorous relationships (Taormino 2008; Veaux and Rickert 2014), the socio-political significance of polyamory (Rambukkana 2015; Schippers 2016; Willey 2016), and there is a growing body of research on poly-amorists, polyamorous relationships, and polyamorous families (Pallotta-Chiarolli 2010; Sheff 2014).

While the poly gaze can offer insight into representations of polyamory per se, in *Polyamory, Monogamy, and American Dreams*, the *poly* in "poly relationships" also includes relationships in which no one identifies as a polyamorist or calls the relationship polyamory. Poly refers to relationships between more than two adults who feel an affinity toward or kinship with each other, and they share some kind of mutual, if temporary, interdependence and responsibility. In other words, the label poly, as I'm using it, identifies a *relationship structure with particular features*, not an identity, subculture, or label adopted by people to distinguish their relationships from other kinds of relationships.

One of the goals in this book, then, is to identify and reveal *poly resonances*. To develop the concept *poly resonances*, I am building on the groundbreaking work of Przybylo and Cooper (2014) on archiving asexual resonances. Describing their project, they write, "we are attuned less to self-identified asexual figures than to asexual 'resonances'—or traces, touches instances—allowing us to search for asexuality in unexpected places" (298). In a similar way, I am not searching for polyamorists in the media texts I cover here, but instead for poly moments, resonances, and attachments in order to search for poly relating in unexpected places. Przybylo and Cooper (2014) go on to say, "Such a queer broadening of what can 'count' as asexuality, especially historically speaking, creates space for unorthodox and unpredictable understandings and manifestations of asexuality" (298). I follow their lead, but instead of focusing on asexuality, I will focus on broadening what "counts" as poly configurations of kinship, attachment, commitment, and desire in order to identify what poly resonances do in the stories we tell about relationships.

Despite my shift from asexuality to poly relationships, I will not completely jettison Przybylo and Cooper's focus on asexuality. I am compelled by their suggestion that we, as queer and feminist theorists, must search for these moments and resonances of asexuality in order to rethink the centrality of sex in feminist and queer theory, and that "queerness should be reworked and rethought from asexual perspectives" (298). Taking their suggestion seriously, I will argue that contemporary definitions of polyamory rely too heavily on romance and sex. By including representations of asexual or non-romantic poly relationships in my analysis, I hope to encourage others to imagine that poly connections and interdependencies show up in all kinds of relationships, not just between romantic partners and lovers. Ela Przybylo writes of her poly relationships:

> My most meaningful community formations have also been poly-asexual, though tense with affective togetherness. Asexuality manifests itself in the premium I place on friendships, broadly understood, as well as on myself. In this sense asexuality multiplies and configures relationship formations.
>
> *(Przybylo and Cooper 2014: 297)*

By including representations of poly-asexual relationships under the rubric of poly relationships, especially in my discussion of queer poly narratives, I hope to expand what we mean when we speak of representations of poly relationships.

Przybylo and Cooper (2014) conclude by saying, "Only through reading asexually can we expand and newly trouble queer understandings of intimacy, polyamory, partnership, kinship, and singleness and also trace asexuality in unexpected, and perhaps even undesirable, locations" (304). By incorporating Przybylo and Cooper's call to engage in a "queerly asexual reading strategy" (299), the poly gaze is very much about reading poly-queerly in ways that expand and trouble queer understandings of intimacy and kinship.

The poly gaze and reading queerly

In his classic text in queer media studies, *Making Everything Perfectly Queer: Interpreting Mass Culture*, Alexander Doty argues for reading media texts and popular culture through a queer lens. Describing the relationship between queerness and media, Doty writes,

> the queerness of mass culture develops in three areas: (1) influences during the production of texts; (2) historically specific cultural readings and uses of texts by self-identified gays, lesbians, bisexuals, queers; and (3) adopting reception positions that can be considered "queer" in some way, regardless of a person's declared sexual and gender allegiances.
>
> *(Doty 1993: xi)*

Queer readings are concerned with who produces texts, who is interpreting them, and how adopting a specifically queer interpretive lens can reveal queerness in texts that are not necessarily produced by or for gay, lesbian, bisexual, trans, or queer audiences.

Reading queerly as developed by Doty is a conscious and cultivated interpretive standpoint available to anyone. In this book, I develop the conceptual tools with which anyone, regardless of their social location or familiarity with polyamory can adopt a poly gaze to see poly resonances. Furthermore, according to Doty, any text is available for queer reading, and reading queerly is no less valid or accurate than other kinds of readings. He writes,

> Queer readings aren't "alternative" readings, wishful or willful misreadings, or "reading too much into things" readings. They result from the recognition and articulation of the complex range of queerness that has been in popular culture texts and their audiences all along.
>
> *(Doty 1993: 16)*

In a similar vein, the poly gaze is concerned with recognizing the complex range of poly resonances that have been in media texts of all sorts all along.

Queer theorists focus on intimate relationships as political and ideological constructs (e.g. Ahmed 2006; Halberstam 2005; Rubin 1984; Warner 1999) and media representations of LGBTQ characters and relationships as reinforcing or challenging heteronormativity (see Rodriguez 2019 for a review of this literature). The monogamous couple as an ideal and institutionalized norm for intimate relationships is a central feature of heteronormativity (Schippers 2016), homonormativity (Duggan 2003; Puar 2007), and definitions of U.S. citizenship

(Berlant and Warner 1998; Warner 1999). Despite this, most critically queer engagements with media representations have, for the most part, left out an analysis of monogamy and mononormativity (Kean 2015). As guest editors for a special issue on queer media in the journal *In Focus*, Ahn, Himberg, and Young (2014) write, "A queer approach to media theory and practice has suggested possibilities for challenging—through critical analysis—overlapping structures of patriarchy, nationhood, citizenship, heteronormativity, and the machinations of neoliberal capitalism" (119). The poly gaze, then, reads queerly in that it reveals how media representations of monogamy as moral and non-monogamy or poly relationships as immoral are deeply embedded within and constitutive of heteronormative notions of intimacy, family, citizenship, and morality. In this way, the poly gaze expands queer media studies by combining an eye for seeing poly resonances with a sociological analytic lens for unpacking the deeper social and cultural meanings conveyed in those moments.

The poly gaze and reading sociologically

According to sociologist Stuart Hall (1997), "we give things meaning by how we represent them—the words we use about them, the stories we tell about them, the images of them we produce, the emotions we associate with them, the ways we classify and conceptualize them, and the values we place on them" (3). The stories collectively told through media representations about intimate relationships, including poly lives, are embedded within and constitutive of collective beliefs and values. Collective beliefs and values are important sociologically because they provide legitimating rationales for setting up social structure including how resources are distributed, which groups are considered valued members of society, and who is understood as having a legitimate claim to authority. Media representations and the stories we tell maintain or sometimes reconfigure dominant narratives about what it means to have intimate relationships, foment kinship ties, and build families. One way to read texts about intimate life from a sociological perspective would be, then, identifying how the implicit and explicit messages, images, and meanings conveyed by the text resonate with or work against prevailing meanings and structures of inequality.

The stories told about intimacy, kinship, and family in U.S. popular culture and other media are, with few and isolated exceptions, decidedly mononormative in that they consistently portray monogamous coupling as the very definition of happily-ever-after (Saxey 2010) and non-monogamy, including polyamory, as titillating but also difficult and dangerous (Antalffi 2011; Corey 2017; Ritchie 2010). For instance, Esther Saxey (2010) identifies how fictional narratives are often pre-occupied with non-monogamy as triangulation, temptation, and/or threat. Although these representations offer a glimpse of monogamy as complicated if not vexed, according to Saxey's analysis, the main function of non-monogamy's presence is to pose a problem in need of solution rather than a viable way to have relationships. Saxey (2010) concludes, "Because monogamy is conflicted and negotiated in these texts, the reader is consistently engaged in a debate; invited to weigh the evidence, assess the worth of sexual options, and (almost invariably) eventually encouraged to dismiss every option but monogamy" (32). Representations of non-monogamy as immoral, unnatural, undesirable, or potentially dangerous are also present in journalism (Antalffi 2011; Mint 2010) and in scientific research (Conley *et al.* 2017; Willey 2016). In a mononormative world, we are surrounded by mononormative stories about non-monogamy and poly relationships, and they are often *morality narratives* that endorse monogamy and de-legitimize poly relationships.

When representations of and narratives about relationships convey the message that monogamous coupling is the key to happiness and non-monogamy is impossible, immature, or dangerous, it steers us toward monogamous coupling as the path to living a happy life. Feminist and queer theorist, Sara Ahmed (2010) adopts a feminist skepticism toward happiness narratives that steer us toward what is presumed to make us happy.

> We learn from this history how happiness is used as a technology or instrument, which allows the reorientation of individual desire toward a common good. We...learn from rereading books...how happiness is not simply used to secure social relationship instrumentally but works as an idea or aspiration within everyday life, shaping the very terms through which individuals share their world with others, creating "scripts" for how to live well.
>
> *(Ahmed 2010: 59)*

One of those scripts orients us toward monogamous coupling as a common good and the key to living well and being happy. Ahmed (2010) writes, "Happiness involves a form of orientation: the very hope for happiness means we get directed in specific ways, as happiness is assumed to follow from some life choices and not others" (54). These scripts often convey and endorse the collective belief in contemporary U.S. culture that the path to good citizenship and happily-ever-after is paved by heterosexual, monogamous coupling (Kipnis 2003; Warner 1999).

The stories we collectively tell also matter sociologically in that they have an effect on how we understand our own place in the social world. Focusing specifically on sexual identities and the coming out stories of lesbian, gay, and bisexually identified people, Kenneth Plummer (1994) suggests that collective and shared storytelling is an important social process by which the gay, lesbian, and bisexual people in his sample develop a sense of identity and political consciousness about what it means to be queer in a heteronormative world. The gay and lesbian participants had to develop new and different stories about intimacy and kinship because the ones told in the mainstream about living a good life dismissed, denigrated, or excluded them. According to Plummer, embracing a queer identity and queer life necessitates telling and sharing new stories about what it means to live a queer life. As a queer, feminist sociologist living a poly life, I am interested in exploring what stories are being told about poly lives and how they do or don't resonate with mononormative assumptions about intimacy, kinship, and family. By searching for poly resonances in unexpected places, I hope to identify when representations or stories about poly relationships are dismissive or denigrating and when they offer new stories about poly relationships that could be perhaps taken up as an alternative way to form intimate connections with others.

Finally, a sociological analysis of the stories told about poly lives means adopting a poly gaze to parse what texts say about who is portrayed as being a good citizen and living a happy life. The stories about who is "happy" and who is deserving of "the good life" give meaning to good, moral, and deserving citizenship. What we will see in the chapters that follow is that narratives about poly lives are often stories about *who* is deserving of happiness. Some of the stories told about poly relationships are cautionary tales of why straying from monogamy is immature, immoral, or perilous, but others offer an implicit endorsement of poly connections and relationships. By paying close attention to which groups are portrayed as naturally monogamous or capable of polyamory and which ones are not, the poly gaze can shed light on how the stories we tell about intimate relationships are embedded within and reproductive of already circulating discourses about race, gender, class, religion, nation, and other systems of inequality.

The poly gaze, then, is not only concerned with how narratives produce and sustain mononormative assumptions about intimacy; it is also a conceptual lens with which one can see how the stories we tell about poly relationships and polyamory resonate with heteronormativity and hegemonic constructions of gender, race, religion, ethnicity, class, and nationalism. This requires analyzing how the stories told about poly lives (whether positive or negative) reproduce hegemonic constructions of social difference and legitimize hierarchies or how, in some cases, they challenge, destabilize, or reconfigure them. Focusing on how the stories we collectively tell about happiness are shot through with gender norms, Sara Ahmed writes:

> We can think of gendered scripts as "happiness scripts" providing a set of instructions for what women and men must do in order to be happy, whereby happiness is what follows being natural or good. Going along with happiness scripts is how we get along: to get along is to be willing and able to express happiness in proximity to the right things.
>
> *(Ahmed 2010: 59)*

In this book I am interested in thinking about how texts about poly lives are at once *relationship* scripts and happiness scripts. They tell us what kinds of relationships are natural and good and *who* succeeds or fails at following those scripts. What we shall see as we move forward is that the relationship scripts told in narratives about poly lives are also stories about gender, race, class, ethnicity, citizenship, religion, and sexuality.

In sum, the poly gaze begins with, but does not end with identifying mono-normativity in the stories told about poly lives. To be sure, the poly gaze is concerned with how representations of poly lives cast monogamy as the key to happiness and living a good life. However, it also asks whether or not and how the stories we tell about poly lives reflect, maintain, and legitimize broader relations of inequality. As we adopt the poly gaze to analyze the texts in this book, we are compelled to ask the following two questions: What is the text saying about poly relationships and happiness, morality, and living the "good life"? In its representation of poly relationships, does the narrative do cultural and ideological work to maintain and legitimize social inequalities along the lines of race, ethnicity, nation, religion, class, gender, and sexuality or does it challenge them?

By way of illustration, I will now move to adopting the poly gaze to offer a poly-queer reading of a film that could not, in any possible way, be read as a movie about polyamory. The film is *Catching Fire* (Lawrence 2013), the second in the four-part (film) series, *The Hunger Games*. My goal is to first shine a light on the poly resonances in the film. I then offer a sociological analysis of what the poly resonances in the plot do to gender and class relations between the characters as they unfold in the film. Finally, I will contextualize *Catching Fire* within the film series in its entirety to show how poly resonances are silenced by the end of the story. The poly gaze, as I will demonstrate, provides a useful conceptual framework for seeing this mononormative turn *and* analyzing how gender and class are established or transformed as a result of the narrative taking this turn.

Reading *Catching Fire* and *The Hunger Games* series with a poly gaze

As I walked out of a theatre after having seen *Catching Fire* (Lawrence 2013), the second film in the *The Hunger Games*, I heard a man say to what I presumed to be his girlfriend or wife, "Why didn't Katniss just pick one or the other? What a slut." The man's comment wasn't surprising—who hasn't heard a man call a woman a slut because she is dating more than one man? The comment, however, did jar me out of my own poly moment, as it were. By poly moment, I mean the relatively rare but significant times when I "see" a poly resonance in the vast sea of monogamous coupling that is contemporary American, popular culture.

If you've seen the film, you might or might not have already guessed why I had such a pleasurable poly moment. *The Hunger Games* is a four-part film series based on a trilogy of novels written by Suzanne Collins. It is a science-fiction dystopian story that takes place in the ruins of the United States. Each year, The Capitol chooses one teenager from each of 12 districts to compete in the Hunger Games. The "game" is a competition for survival, with only one teenager claiming victory after killing the rest. There are very clear class differences between the wealthy Capitol and the citizens of the districts, and citizens of The Capitol do not participate in the Games but act as titillated spectators. The four films follow Katniss Everdeen and her allies as they resist the Capitol.

FIGURE 1.1 Katniss and Gale share their first kiss
Source: *The Hunger Games: Catching Fire* 2013.

In the film *Catching Fire*, the main protagonist, Katniss Everdeen, acknowledges her dependence on, love for, and commitment to two men, Peeta and Gale. By the end of the film, and much to my delight, she chooses neither and instead forms romantic and political alliances with both. Although Peeta and Gale are not happy about the situation, they agree to the arrangement and remain in the poly relationship with Katniss and with each other throughout the entire film. Though it is clear that neither Peeta nor Gale are comfortable, it is significant from my poly perspective that 1) they agree to go along, and 2) the film did not end with mononormative closure.

Moreover, their mutual interdependence and sense of responsibility to each other and their affective ties bind them together as three and in ways that extend

FIGURE 1.2 Katniss takes care of and protects Peeta when he is injured during the Games
Source: *The Hunger Games* 2012.

beyond romance and sexual desire—they need each other to survive, and they are political allies. As romance and sexual desire recede as the tie that binds, political alliances based on class consciousness come to the fore. They remain allies until the end *and* romantic or sexual desire between Katniss and Gale and Peeta is still present. However, their political alliance, not their romantic feelings or sexual desire, is the most salient feature of their bonds at the end of the film. We might say that, at the end of this film, their bonds include poly-asexual resonances. This representation of asexual bonds along the lines of class and in opposition to the Capitol is one example of how the stories we tell about poly lives could also be stories about political alliances. In my poly reading, their poly relationship resonates with their class allegiances rather than, as is the case in most narratives of love triangles (Sedgwick 1985), potentially destroying their class alliance. In other words, while it's possible to interpret the "love triangle" between Katniss, Peeta, and Gale as a sexual and/or romantic subplot, I read it poly-queerly. At the end of *Catching Fire*, Katniss is less *torn* between two lovers and more *tied* to two allies who share her political and economic class interests. In this film, poly triangulation is not a problem to be solved; it is necessary for survival.

The poly resonances in *Catching Fire* also provide interpretive space to read gender in poly-queer ways. As I have argued elsewhere (Schippers 2016), the poly structure of the relationship between Katniss, Peeta, and Gale in *Catching Fire* opens up a narrative path for Katniss to embody both masculinity and femininity and for Peeta to embody femininity. In the words of NPR film critic, Linda Holmes (2013), Katniss is the Movie Boyfriend and Peeta is the Movie Girlfriend. For instance, when Katniss interacts with Peeta, she is a more competent warrior than he is, and she often takes charge and protects him. She occupies what might be considered the masculine role in relationship to Peeta, who plays the feminine part. In contrast, when Katniss is with Gale, she occupies a more feminine role by letting him lead and, instead of protecting him, she offers emotional support and nurtures him when he is injured. Because she maintains her relationship with both throughout the film—because she, Peeta, and Gale are in a relationship with poly resonances—we see many different facets to her character and, as a result, her character is more complex and well rounded.

The poly resonances in *Catching Fire* open up narrative space for representations of gender that challenge rather than reproduce assumptions about masculinity, femininity, and who is allowed to be The Movie Girlfriend and The Movie Boyfriend. If, on the other hand, the narrative led to Katniss choosing one over the other, as the man coming out of the theatre had hoped, the character would have had to jettison parts of herself in order to make her choosing one and rejecting the other make sense. In other words, the mononormative prescription to love and commit to one and only one man would force Katniss to, not only "choose" a partner, but also to choose a gender—for herself.

Unfortunately, this is where Katniss lands by the end of the fourth and last film in *The Hunger Games*. Despite the film *Catching Fire* having poly resonances, *The Hunger Games* series, in its entirety, is a mononormative narrative. A mononormative

FIGURE 1.3 Katniss holds her and Peeta's child as she gazes lovingly at him
Source: *The Hunger Games: Mockingjay – Part 2* 2015.

narrative, remember, is one that assumes or insists that monogamous coupling is moral, desirable, and the path to happiness and a good life. The last scene in *Mockingjay-Part 2* (Lawrence 2015) depicts Katniss tending to her children while Peeta stands guard. Although Katniss, Peeta, and Gale were in a poly relationship at the end of *Catching Fire*, in the final scene of the entire story Gale is completely out of the picture, and Katniss has, apparently, chosen Peeta. This closing scene portrays the heterosexual, monogamous couple with children as the very definition of a happy ending.

The narrative construction of monogamous marriage with one man and dependent children as "happily-ever-after" is decidedly mononormative *and* heteronormative. It reinforces mononormativity by perpetuating the idea that poly relationships are temporary rather than a viable and happy state of affairs. This is particularly ironic given the film series is a story about class struggle and perseverance in the face of oppression and annihilation. Despite the *class-based* trials and tribulations Katniss, Peeta, and Gale experienced over the four films and Katniss's political commitments, the monogamous hetero-patriarchal family happy ending erases class completely. The poly resonances found in *Catching Fire* are completely silenced, which means class alliances between the three characters are reduced to heteronormative ties that bind us to gender normalcy.

Furthermore, by narrating Katniss into the patriarchal family, the story forces Katniss (and Peeta) to choose either the masculine role or the feminine role. In the final scene we see her passively sitting in the grass watching the children while Peeta stands and watches for danger. Katniss is portrayed as nurturing, not courageous, and she and her children are protected by Peeta. Peeta is no longer vulnerable and incapable. Instead he has become the masculine protector and leader. The story binds monogamy, gender conformity, and the patriarchal family structure into a tight package of living happily-ever-after. By doing so, *The Hunger Games* encourages a sort of cruel optimism about the heterosexual, patriarchal nuclear family as the ultimate path to happiness. Lauren Berlant (2011) writes:

Cruel optimism…is an incitement to inhabit and to track the affective attachment to what we call "the good life," which is for so many a bad life that wears out the subjects who nonetheless, and at the same time, find their conditions of possibility within it.

(27)

The "American Dream" and American media are saturated with this cruel optimism about monogamous coupling, happiness, and the heteronormative, patriarchal family. Many of the stories we tell encourage us to see monogamous coupling in heteronormative families as the only or best way to get our needs met. More important, by establishing hetero-patriarchal family as narrative closure, the series de-politicizes all of the characters and renders the plot around class oppression and struggle secondary to family, procreation, and traditional gender roles. If the poly resonances were carried through to the end, one could imagine that poly kinship, class alliances, and gender equality could have been a different kind of happy ending.

Of course, my poly reading of *Catching Fire* and *The Hunger Games* is not the only or even "correct" interpretation. Not everyone who sees the films will read *Catching Fire* as having poly resonances or the trilogy as mononormative. The man I overheard walking out of the theatre, for instance, didn't see a poly relationship; he saw an immoral woman stringing two men along. The man's assertion that Katniss was a slut for not choosing either Peeta or Gale was grounded in a fundamental assumption that moral characters, especially women, end up in monogamous couple relationships. From his mono perspective, the three-way dynamic was a tension in need of resolution, not a happy state of affairs as I saw it. My guess is that he was quite pleased with how *Mockingjay-Part 2* ended.

This is why I believe it is important to offer the poly gaze as a new way to read media texts. Texts are *polysemic*, meaning they can have multiple meanings and different people will interpret narratives in varied ways (Hall 1980). Readers and audiences bring their own social and cultural meanings to the process of interpretation, and so, reception of media is not a simple and passive absorption of the messages conveyed; it is an active process. Whether or not one reads texts poly-queerly will partially depend on whether or not a viewer has a conscious awareness of mononormativity and has an interest in finding poly resonances in unexpected places. This book is an invitation to both. As an alternative to the preferred or dominant mononormative reading, I hope to offer a different kind of reading practice. As I will show in the following chapters, *Catching Fire* is not the only media text that features poly resonances. There are poly things going on in all kinds of texts from television, film, and journalism to historical biographies and social science research. *Polyamory, Monogamy, and American Dreams* invites readers to come along as I adopt a poly gaze to 1) bring poly resonances to the fore and, at the same time, 2) identify the sociological significance of the stories and narratives told about poly lives.

Finally, although I am not aware of any other poly readings of *Catching Fire* and *The Hunger Games*, I am certainly not the first to write about representations of poly relationships in media and popular culture. For instance, Sam See (2004) adopts what I am calling a poly gaze to read the Noel Coward play, *Design for Living*, as a narrative about a poly relationship between two bisexual men and a woman rather than, as many culture critics suggested, a story about two, closeted, gay men. See's reading reveals the sociological significance of *Design for Living* by analyzing the ways in which the portrayal of a polyamorous triad challenges mononormativity, but also makes bisexuality visible. Bisexual visibility is a common theme in poly readings of popular culture. In her analysis of the film *French Twist*, Serena Anderlini-D'Onofrio (2009) suggests that poly narratives that include three people opens up narrative space for a character to simultaneously love more than one gender. Anderlini-D'Onofrio (2009) writes:

> [*French Twist*] provides the context to prove that, once the cultural restrictions due to monogamy and monosexuality are lifted, happy endings turn into open structures that can discursively and/or factually include the third party who has in some ways been the vehicle for the desire between the two players in the conventional couple.
>
> *(344)*

Similarly, Natasa Pivec (2018) offers an analysis of the German film, *Three*, which is, according to Pivec, representative of "polyamory-oriented cinema that is… invested into representing polyamorous stories accurately and realistically" (85). Rather than depicting polyamory as adultery or as indicative of a gay character's refusal to come out of the closet, *Three* portrays polyamory as a viable relationship form in its own right and as a vehicle for making bisexual desire and identifications visible. Drawing a connection between the importance of positive representations of LGBTQ characters, Pivec (2018) suggests that the same holds for stories about polyamory.

> [W]hat *Three* and future films about non-monogamies can do is what lesbian and gay cinema facilitated for LGBT+ folks: visibility, recognition, acceptance, familiarisation, normalisation and "de-Otherness" in general. As have LGBT+ cinematic representations changed over time—from demonization to acceptance—so can polyamorous cinema, with films like *Three* changing the narrative about dyadic love to endorse other types of intimacy.
>
> *(94–95)*

These and other studies do significant work to challenge mononormativity and identify poly themes and relationships in media. My intention is to follow rather than challenge their lead by doing the same. However, at the same time, my hope is that *Polyamory, Monogamy, and American Dreams* goes deeper and wider by developing the poly gaze as a *method* for reading queerly. The chapters that follow provide, by way of example, a conceptual framework with which anyone can see poly resonances (including but not limited to romantic and sexual, polyamorous relationships) and analyze their sociological significance as collective meaning-making.

Summary of chapters

In this book, my goal is to revisit and interpret texts with a poly gaze. I do not empirically research Fundamentalist Church of Latter Day Saints (FLDS) polygamy or campus hookup cultures. Instead, I analyze how journalists and researchers talk about polygamy and hookup cultures. For instance, in the next chapter, "The Polygamous Other and American Identity," I adopt the poly gaze to analyze narratives told in the mainstream media about the practice of polygyny by members of the FLDS. I begin by reviewing the works of several authors who identify how historical and contemporary gender narratives about Mormon polygamy reify monogamy as superior to any other relationship structure and, by doing so, uphold colonial and imperialist constructions of Northern European cultures as superior, more advanced, and modern and render U.S. and Canadian nation states as white, Christian, and gender egalitarian. I then adopt the poly gaze to provide a close reading of John Krakauer's (2004) best-selling book, *Under the Banner of Heaven: A Story of Violent Faith*. I argue that by obsessively focusing on polygamy and religion rather than gender and the criminalization of polygamy, Krakauer's narrative reproduces narratives about U.S. citizenship, gender, religion, and race. I show how Krakauer consistently conflates polygamy (plural marriage) with backward, rural religiosity and with male dominance. Implicitly, he articulates the Western construction of Christian, monogamous marriage as inherently gender egalitarian and as more civilized than polygamy. In so doing, Krakauer reproduces rather than challenges colonial-imperialist narratives that construct the "polygamous other" as un-American and uncivilized. The poly gaze will reveal that Krakauer's narrative is mononormative to be sure. He completely ignores or is unaware of research literature that empirically documents forms of plural marriage in the FLDS that are not abusive to women and children. Moreover, Krakauer's inability to see any alternative to monogamous, dyadic marriage makes *Under the Banner of Heaven* a book not only about polygamy, but also about gender, class, and citizenship.

In Chapter 3, "Casual Sex On Campus: The Mononormative Narratives Told About Sexual Relationships in Heterosexual Hookup Cultures," I adopt a poly gaze to analyze the ways in which researchers talk about casual sex, relationships, and gender inequality in heterosexual campus hookup cultures. The poly gaze reveals that researchers often articulate the very same mononormative assumptions about relationships that are circulating in hookup culture. By assuming that sexual exclusivity defines relationships and that monogamous coupling is the only other option besides casually hooking up, researchers not only perpetuate mononormativity, they also reinforce rather than critically examine the unequal gender dynamics in heterosexual campus hookup cultures.

Chapter 4, "Historical Biography and The Erasure of Poly Pasts" is an exploration of contemporary, historical biographies about people who were committed to "free love," practiced consensual non-monogamy, or were involved in what appear to be poly relationships. I am not a historical biographer so instead of writing historical biography, I analyze historical biographies as text to identify how they construct poly lives. I highlight the poly resonances in each biography and analyze how the biographers interpret and describe those resonances. I show that, by rendering consensual non-monogamy and poly intimacies invisible, strange, or the source of strife, biographers often erase the political significance of living a poly life for their subjects. I conclude that this erasure or dismissal of poly ways of living constructs a mononormative history of human relationships, and it renders invisible the relationship between a radical gender, race, sexual, and/or class politics and the rejection of compulsory monogamy.

In Chapters 5 and 6 my focus shifts from mononormative narratives about poly lives and toward poly narratives. I analyze films and television shows from a sociological perspective to situate them within broader cultural narratives about citizenship and living a good life. In Chapter 5, "Poly-Positive Narratives and American Sexual Exceptionalism," I turn the poly gaze on two films, *Savages* and *Splendor*, as exemplary of *polynormative narratives*. I will show how, while both films offer positive or sympathetic representations of polyamory, they rely upon hegemonic constructions of gender, race, class, nation, and sexuality to render polyamory normal but also as evidence of American sexual exceptionalism (Puar 2007).

In Chapter 6, "The (Poly) Love That Dare Not Speak Its Name: Poly Kinship as a Design for Living Queerly," I use a poly gaze to explore *polyqueer narratives* or stories about poly relationships that rewrite, reconfigure, and queer the meaning of happiness, the good life, and security. I argue that these polyqueer narratives are not "about" polyamory per se but instead offer representations of non-dyadic sex, relationships, or kinship in ways that challenge rather than reproduce heteronormativity.

Finally, I close the book with a brief discussion of the significance of the poly gaze in the contemporary U.S. political and cultural climate. Shifting from analysis to a kind of speculative rumination, I wonder about how *thinking* poly might change our affective orientation in the realm of political organizing and activism. I suggest that finding paths of transformation rather than assimilation is especially imperative within the contemporary context of the material deterioration of family security under the pressures of austerity, a political culture that defines belonging by establishing boundaries around the family (excluding queers) and nation (excluding immigrants), and the rise of neo-fascism in the United States and Europe.

Before we move on to the chapters summarized above, however, I want to say something about the scope of this book. First, it is wholly focused on texts produced in contemporary U.S. culture. While this prevents me from speaking to mononormativity and polynormativity in other cultural contexts, my analytic focus is on how American stories about polyamory and poly relationships are embedded within and feed U.S. global imperialism and American exceptionalism. Also, while the content of my analysis is bound to contemporary U.S. culture, my hope is that the sociological analytic framework connecting narratives about relationships to broader systems of inequality might be useful in other cultural contexts.

Second, I limit my focus to certain textual forms and genres and do not provide analyses of others. For instance, I do not analyze popular music, art, theatre, dance, political speeches, or social media. All of these are important places in which stories about monogamy, polyamory, and social inequality might be told and thus are in need of analysis with a poly gaze. To state the obvious, it would be beyond the scope of this (or any) book to cover all texts and all forms of narrative. This book reflects my own interests, tastes, and expertise. Despite the limited scope of the kinds of texts analyzed here, I hope that, after having read *Polyamory, Monogamy, and American Dreams*, others might be encouraged and conceptually equipped to adopt a poly gaze to interpret any cultural text or narrative regardless of its content or form.

Note

1 As a sociologist, I am less interested in the psychological processes with which people experience desire as they read cultural texts, and more interested in the texts themselves and what they can tell us about culture. However, I do believe that there is important work to be done on the workings of mononormativity in these processes and on how representations of non-dyadic sex and relationships might alter or confound these processes.

References

Ahn, Patty, Julia Himberg, and Damon R. Young. 2014. "Introduction: Queer Approaches to Film, Television, and Digital Media." *In Focus* 53(2): 117–121.

Ahmed, Sara. 2006. *Queer Phenomenology: Orientations, Objects, Others*. Durham, NC: Duke University Press.

Ahmed, Sara. 2010. *The Promise of Happiness*. Durham, NC: Duke University Press.

Anapol, Deborah. 2010. *Polyamory in the 21st Century: Love and Intimacy with Multiple Partners*. New York: Rowman and Littlefield.

Anderlini-D'Onofrio, Serena. 2009. "Plural Happiness: Bi and Poly Triangulations in Balasko's French Twist." *Journal of Bisexuality* 9(3–4): 343–361.

Antalffi, Nikó. 2011. "Polyamory and the Media." *Scan: Journal of Media Arts Culture*. Online Journal of the Department of Media, Music, Communication and Cultural Studies at Macquarie University, Sydney. http://scan.net.au/scn/journal.html.

Berlant, Lauren. 2011. *Cruel Optimism*. Durham, NC: Duke University Press.

Berlant, Lauren and Michael Warner. 1998. "Sex in Public." *Critical Inquiry* 24(2): 547–566.

Conley, T. D., Matsick, J. L., Moors, A. C., and Ziegler, A. 2017. "Investigation of Consensually Nonmonogamous Relationships: Theories, Methods, and New Directions." *Perspectives on Psychological Science* 12(2), 205–232.

Corey, Sarah. 2017. "All Bi Myself: Analyzing Television's Presentation of Female Bisexuality." *Journal of Bisexuality* 17(2): 190–205.

Doty, Alexander. 1993. *Making Things Perfectly Queer: Interpreting Mass Culture*. Minneapolis: University of Minnesota Press.

Duggan, Lisa. 2003. *The Twilight of Equality? Neoliberalism, Cultural Politics, and The Attack on Democracy*. New York: Beacon.

Easton, Dossie and Janet W. Hardy. 2009. *The Ethical Slut: A Practical Guide to Polyamory, Open Relationships, and Other Adventures*, 2nd edn. Berkeley, CA: Celestial Arts.

Halberstam, J. 2005. *In a Queer Time and Place: Transgender Bodies, Subcultural Lives*. New York: New York University Press.

Hall, Stewart. 1980. "Encoding / Decoding." In Hall, S., D. Hobson, A. Lowe, and P. Willis (Eds), *Culture, Media, Language: Working Papers in Cultural Studies, 1972–79*. London: Hutchinson, 128–138.

Hall, Stuart. 1997. *Representation: Cultural Representations and Signifying Practices*. London: Sage.

Holmes, Linda. 2013. "What Really Makes Katniss Stand Out? Peeta, Her Movie Girlfriend." https://www.npr.org/2013/11/25/247146164/what-really-makes-katniss-stand-out-peeta-her-movie-girlfriend.

Kean, Jessica. 2015. "A Stunning Plurality: Unravelling Hetero- and Mononormativities through HBO's *Big Love*." *Sexualities* 18(5/6): 698–713.

Kipnis, Laura. 2003. *Against Love: A Polemic*. New York: Vintage.

Krakauer, John. 2004. *Under the Banner of Heaven: A Story of Violent Faith*. New York: Anchor.

Lawrence, Francis. 2013. *Catching Fire* [Film]. Los Angeles: Lionsgate.

Lawrence, Francis. 2015. *Mockingjay-Part 2* [Film]. Los Angeles: Lionsgate.

Mint, Pepper. 2010. "The Power Mechanisms of Jealousy." In Meg Barker and Darren Langdridge (Eds), *Understanding Non-Monogamies*. New York: Routledge, 201–206.

Pallotta-Chiarolli, M. 2010. *Border Sexualities, Border Families in Schools*. New York: Rowman & Littlefield.

Pivec, Natasa. 2018. "'Three (Is Not a Crowd)': An Analysis of Tom Tykwer's Polyamorous Film Three." *Graduate Journal of Social Science* 14(1): 79–99.

Plummer, Ken. 1994. *Telling Sexual Stories: Power, Change and Social Worlds*. New York: Routledge.

Przybylo, Ela and Danielle Cooper. 2014. "Asexual Resonances: Tracing a Queerly Asexual Archive." *GLQ: A Journal of Lesbian and Gay Studies* 20(3): 297–318.

Puar, Jasbir. 2007. *Terrorist Assemblages: Homonationalism in Queer Times*. Durham, NC: Duke University Press.

Rambukkana, Nathan. 2015. *Fraught Intimacies: Non-Monogamy in the Public Sphere*. Vancouver: UBC Press.

Ritchie, Ani. 2010. "Discursive Constructions of Polyamory in Mononormative Media Culture." In Meg Barker and Darren Langdridge (Eds), *Understanding Non-Monogamies*. New York: Routledge, 46–53.

Ritchie, Ani and Meg Barker. 2006. "'There Aren't Words for What We Do or How We Feel So We Have to Make Them Up': Constructing Polyamorous Languages in a Culture of Compulsory Monogamy." *Sexualities* 9(5): 584–601.

Rodriguez, Julian A. 2019. "Lesbian, Gay, Bisexual, Transgender, and Queer Media: Key Narratives, Future Directions." *Sociological Compass* 13(4): 1–10.

Rubin, Gayle. 1984. "Thinking Sex: Notes for a Radical Theory of the Politics of Sexuality." In Carole S. Vance (Ed), *Pleasure and Danger: Exploring Female Sexuality*. London: Pandora.

Saxey, Esther. 2010. "Non-Monogamy and Fiction." In Meg Barker and Darren Langdridge (Eds), *Understanding Non-Monogamies*. New York: Routledge, 23–33.

Sedgwick, Eve Kosofsky. 1985. *Between Men: English Literature and Male Homosocial Desire.* New York: Columbia University Press.

Schippers, Mimi. 2016. "Compulsory Monogamy in The Hunger Games." In Lisa Wade, Douglas Hartmann, and Christopher Uggen (Eds), *Assigned: Life with Gender.* New York: W.W. Norton & Company.

See, Sam. 2004. "Other Kitchen Sinks, Other Drawing rooms: Radical Designs for Living in Pre-1968 British Drama." *Journal of Bisexuality* 4(3–4): 29–54.

Sheff, Elisabeth. 2014. *The Polyamorist Next Door: Inside Multiple-Partner Relationships and Families.* New York: Rowman and Littlefield.

Taormino, Tristan. 2008. *Opening Up: a Guide to Creating and Sustaining Open Relationships.* San Francisco, CA: Cleis Press.

Veaux, Franklin and Eve Rickert. 2014. *More Than Two: A Practical Guide to Polyamory.* Portland, OR: Thorntree Press.

Warner, Michael. 1999. *The Trouble with Normal: Sex, Politics, and the Ethics of Queer Life.* Boston, MA: Harvard University Press.

Willey, Angela. 2016. *Undoing Monogamy: The Politics of Science and the Possibilities of Biology.* Durham, NC: Duke University Press.

2

THE POLYGAMOUS OTHER AND AMERICAN IDENTITY

In April 2008, Texas law enforcement agents raided Yearning for Zion (YFZ), a rural community in Eldorado, Texas, inhabited by 800 members of the Fundamentalist Church of Jesus Christ of Latter Day Saints (FLDS). The raid occurred after a caller claiming to be Sarah Jessop, the seventh wife of Dale Barlow, notified police that she and other young girls were being physically and sexually abused and forced into polygamous marriages with older men in the community. Four hundred women and children were taken into Child Welfare custody. It would take two years in court until they were allowed to return to their own homes. Later it was discovered that the call was a hoax, and the caller had connections with an anti-polygamy organization (Wright and Richardson 2011: 1).

Comparing the raid in Eldorado with a raid in 1953 on FLDS members in Short Creek, Utah, Martha Bradley Evans (2011) writes, "In the fifty-five years between 1953 and 2008, Mormon fundamentalism evolved to become a distinctive religious culture that persisted despite considerable efforts by both the federal and state governments to eliminate it" (29). According to Evans, the raids were less about child abuse and more about the practice of plural marriage despite the fact that members of YFZ did not break anti-polygamy laws. Men legally married only their first wife and then were sealed to other wives through, what members of the FLDS call spiritual binding, not legal contract.

> Given the government does not regulate "spiritual" marriage or other forms of intimate private relationships, the elaborate state raids can hardly be justified on legal grounds. Rather, it seems that the state may have substituted the claims of child abuse for the morally offensive practice of plural marriage, taking advantage of both aggressive laws on child protection and the vulnerability of the FLDS, as a separatist community, to this charge.
>
> *(Evans 2011: 47)*

FIGURE 2.1 Local, state, and federal officers round up the women and children from Yearning for Zion
Source: AP Archived Video 2015, accessed June 10, 2019, https://www.youtube.com/watch?v=1hxmws7yQMQ&t=2s.

After reviewing court documents, Evans suggests that, at the time, the evidence of child abuse was sparse and did not appear to be systemic. Despite this, media coverage was "moral theatre" rather than objective coverage of illegal activity, and men of the FLDS were cast as "perverts, pedophiles, and fanatics" (Evans 2011: 46), while women were assumed to be completely brainwashed, lacking agency, complicit, and abusive themselves (Park 2016).

Of course, this is not the first time that a sexual minority has been cast as a danger to children and as morally suspect. LGBT populations have and continue to be constructed as immoral, dangerous, and thus not deserving the rights of citizenship. A review of how mainstream discourses about and actions taken by state and local law enforcement against the FLDS makes clear that polygamy must be included among those dissident and pathologized sexualities (Denike 2010; Park 2016).

Social anxieties, especially in times of rapid social change, are often displaced on to the sexual practices of minority or dissident populations. According to legal scholar Sarah Song (2016), this is precisely the context in which Mormon polygamy became the object of derision in the nineteenth century.

> The broader historical context in which antipolygamy arose was a period of increasing anxiety over sexual values, family structure, and the proper role of women. Social changes in the majority culture—the spread of prostitution, the rising incidence of divorce, and lax morality of the growing cities—stirred anxieties about the preservation of Christian-model monogamy. By the time

the issue of polygamy arose on the national political stage, nineteenth-century women's-rights activists had already been unsettling prevailing gender norms.

(Song 2016: 27–28)

It is not surprising then that the welfare of women and children was and continues to be deployed as a rationale for the prejudice against and persecution of members of the FLDS.

The antipolygamy movement's persistent focus on the theme of sexual perversion allowed members of the majority culture to displace its anxieties about these social changes onto subversive minorities. In addition to its subversive sexual practices, Mormonism's association with lenient divorce laws and female enfranchisement fueled fears that all three were part of a plot to undermine the traditional American family and Christian civilization itself.

(Song 2016: 28)

The conflation of polygamous practices in the FLDS with other crimes like, in the case described above, child sexual abuse and forced marriage, is a pervasive mainstream discourse about the FLDS (Park 2016). Equating plural marriage with child sexual abuse, forced marriage, and women's subordination as if there is something inherent to plural marriage that leads to inequality and abhorrent behavior is a *mononormative discourse*. It falsely equates monogamous marriage with egalitarian gender relations and children's well-being, as if there is something inherently progressive, egalitarian, or more "civilized" about monogamy (Beaman 2016). As I will discuss below, the extent to which the FLDS is disavowed by the mainstream Mormon Church, persecuted by law enforcement, and stereotyped as perverts by the media *because* they practice plural marriage is grounded in very old and deeply Northern European and North American assumptions about the relationship between monogamous marriage, sexuality, and good citizenship.

My goal in this chapter is not to defend the FLDS, advocate for plural marriage, or suggest that "elite polygyny" (Bennion 2016a), where only a handful of elite men are able to marry several wives, is anything but a male dominant structure for marriage. Instead, my focus in this chapter is less on polygamy or the FLDS and more on mononormative discourses *about Mormon polygamy* and the cultural work those discourses do to 1) reify monogamy as superior to any other relationship structure, 2) uphold colonial and imperialist constructions of Northern European cultures as superior, more advanced, and modern, and 3) by doing so, render U.S. and Canadian nation states as white, Christian, and gender egalitarian. Stated another way, I adopt a poly gaze to draw attention to the ways in which narratives about the FLDS in the United States and Canada are deeply mononormative and embedded within and constitutive of broader discourses about the moral superiority of Northern Europe and North America as more democratic, egalitarian, and modern.

Building on the work of others who have written about the persecution of the FLDS in the U.S. context, I will show how representations of the FLDS equate polygamy with criminality, gender inequality, and fanatical religiosity on the one hand and monogamous marriage with moral superiority, civility, and good citizenship on the other. To do so, I will first review the research literature on the history of anti-polygamy law in North America and contemporary sentiments about both Mormon and Muslim polygamy. I will then offer a close reading of the best-selling book, *Under the Banner of Heaven: A Story of Violent Faith* by John Krakauer (2004) to identify how Krakauer reproduces Western constructions of polygamy and paints a rather simplistic caricature of FLDS men as inherently despotic, violent, and oppressive and women who participate in polygamous marriages as passive and brainwashed victims, or, as Park (2016) suggests, a subaltern Other. With a poly lens, I read Krakauer's book as a textual example of U.S. colonial discourses that define Western nations as civilized, rational, progressive, and *monogamous* and the practice of polygamy as primitive, barbaric, and un-American. Moreover, I will argue that, by reproducing these mononormative and simplistic assumptions about polygamy, Krakauer's narrative in *Under the Banner of Heaven* is embedded within and fully articulates these mononormative assumptions about polygamy *and* colonial and imperialist discourses about the superiority of the United States and Western culture more broadly.

The criminalization of polygamy in North America

The persecution of Mormons is nothing new and, as has been documented by several historians, legal scholars, anthropologists, and sociologists, is inextricable from the history of the United States as a patriarchal, white supremacist, settler colonial nation state (see Burgett 2005; Ertman 2010; Klesse 2018).

In the mid-nineteenth century, Mormons moved west to flee prejudice and persecution. The persecution was largely due to their practice of polygyny. Settling in what was then the Utah territory, they established a solid and unified voting block that included women's enfranchisement, economic independence through locally owned businesses and commerce, and a religiously prescribed and institutionalized form of polygynous marriage. The political and economic power of the LDS (Latter Day Saints) posed a significant threat to the expanding U.S. nation state, especially in the context of reconstruction, the first wave of the women's movement, Chinese immigration, and state interests in colonizing western lands. Margaret Denike (2010) suggests that anti-polygamy sentiments are inextricable from "post civil-war anxiety about the naturalness of America's racial and political destiny as a white Christian nation" (855).

Anti-polygamy rhetoric and the criminalization of polygamy were central strategies deployed to dismantle LDS efforts to form a separatist and theocratic nation in Utah. Because LDS women were enfranchised and, with FLDS men, formed a formidable voting block, federal laws denied polygamists the right to vote and hold office. In order to gain voting rights, Mormon men and women had to take an oath swearing they were not polygamists (Song 2016).

During this time, mainstream discourse about polygamy and the LDS relied upon and articulated circulating narratives about Western culture, race, gender, and religion. For instance, one of the central narratives about polygamy was that it was a primitive and barbaric form of marriage practiced by the supposedly less evolved peoples of Africa and Asia. In contrast, the colonial narrative goes, Northern European and North American cultures are more evolved, civilized, democratic, and monogamous (Burgett 2005; Ertman 2010). According to Martha Ertman (2010), legal documents and propaganda in magazines, newspapers, and comics depicted Mormons as having Asian and African physical features and, in the context of pervasive evolutionary and biological theories of the racial superiority of white people of European descent, cast polygamy as a degenerating form of kinship.

In contrast, monogamous marriage was held up as more "civilized" and was assumed to be evidence of human progress with people of Northern European descent leading the way. Religion scholar Lori Beaman (2016) writes, "The male 'Other,' often racialized, associated with wildness and lack of civility or progress, was also identified as being linked to polygamy, continuing an ongoing link between the oriental or racialized 'Other' and the dangers of polygamy" (54). This opened discursive space to cast Mormons as un-American race traitors and a contextually specific and racialized legal argument for the criminalization of polygamy. Ertman (2010) explains,

> Casting overwhelmingly White Mormons as non-White required rhetorical slights of hand. While Mormons' distinctive theology and social organization were politically unsettling in many ways, the practice of polygamy justified the larger culture's demotion of Mormons from full citizenship on the grounds of racial inferiority.
>
> *(2)*

For instance, depictions of Mormons would often include one white man accompanied by several wives of different races, "making the numerosity and miscegenation jokes in the same breath" (Ertman 2010: 11). Just as "scientists" of the time sought anatomical evidence of gender, racial, and sexual hierarchies (Somerville 2000), medical professionals looked for physical indicators of degeneracy in the bodies of polygamists and their children (Ertman 2010).

In addition to constructing racialized narratives about the superiority of Western culture, anti-polygamy discourse was also embedded within nineteenth-century debates about the role of women in marriage and the public sphere. Sarah Song (2016) argues that the "condemnation of polygamy helped divert attention from the majority culture's own patriarchal norms. The focus on polygamy helped shield Christian monogamy and the traditional gender roles associated with it from criticism" (29). She continues,

The [Muslim] harem signified coercion and despotism, whereas monogamy connoted consent and political liberty. The leading political and legal philosophers of the early-American republic contrasted monogamy with polygamy in order to illustrate the superiority of Christian morality over "oriental despotism."

(Song 2016: 29)

This narrative about "oriental polygamy" being authoritarian and anti-democratic and "Christian monogamy" being liberal and "free" depended upon and bolstered the mononormative presumption that monogamy is moral and serves the interests of the state and plural marriage as contrary to state interests.

At the same time, however, Mormon men were depicted as unable to control their wives and children, and thus unable to organize and oversee state authority.

Over and over, antipolygamy cartoons deride plural marriage as a disorderly or backward domestic arrangement, implicitly analogizing household disorder to government disorder. Chaotic domestic scenes depict brawling wives and screaming children while a sidelined husband fails to exercise proper authority over his wives and children by virtue of being outnumbered...Implicitly, these scenes assert that if Mormons cannot govern their households, they cannot properly govern their territory. Some cartoons feature Uncle Sam as a father figure, either disciplining the unruly children (who might signify territories or unpopular groups), or lounging in an armchair when he should be disciplining "problems" like Mormons and Indians for defying federal authority.

(Ertman 2010: 11)

In a white supremacist nation state built upon the political ideology of democracy and the *monogamous*, patriarchal nuclear family, plural marriage was the scaffolding upon which mainstream discourse built a portrait of Mormons as despotic race traitors who did not live up to normative gender expectations. Court decisions leading to the eventual criminalization of polygamy relied upon and further articulated this portrait.

Many Americans, from the highest levels of government to political cartoonists, viewed the Mormons' political treason as part of a larger, even more sinister offense that I call race treason. According to this view, polygamy was natural for people of color, but unnatural for White Americans of Northern European descent...The Supreme Court accepted this argument in the leading antipolygamy case, Reynolds v. United States, in which it rejected Mormon claims that polygamy was protected as the free exercise of religion. The Court reasoned that polygamy was "odious among the northern and western nations of Europe," "almost exclusively a feature of the life of Asiatic and of African people," and ultimately "fetters the people in stationary despotism." Well into the twentieth century, many Americans continued to associate White

Mormons with people of color, as evidenced by a character's quip in Jack London's 1914 novel, "They ain't whites; they're Mormons."

(Ertman 2010: 2)

The characterization of monogamy as white and more civilized and polygamy as something practiced by "primitive" races from Asia and Africa was circulating more broadly in Western colonial discourse (Willey 2016), and it served the expanding U.S. government's persecution of the politically and economically powerful LDS well. Mononormative narratives about the immorality and barbarism of polygamy and superiority of monogamy masked the political and economic motivations of the U.S. nation state to contain and dismantle a rapidly growing and powerful separatist religion and legitimate discrimination against Chinese immigrants, the enslavement of people of African descent, the disenfranchisement of women, and the establishment of Christian Protestantism as the most civilized among the religions. In other words, mononormativity was one of many discourses that established the expanding United States as a white, protestant, patriarchal, and *monogamous* nation-state.

Contemporary anti-polygamy sentiments

The idea that monogamy is more civilized, gender egalitarian, and associated with Western, Christian nations continues into the present. In addition to the journalistic treatment of the raids on FLDS communities described above, contemporary, evolutionary anthropologists also render monogamy more evolved than polygamy (see Symons 1979). Interestingly, even those evolutionary anthropologists who argue that humans evolved to have a propensity for polygamy, still, through rather astonishing twists of logic, manage to reproduce the Western idea that monogamy is more egalitarian, just, and progressive. For example, in his book *Out of Eden*, evolutionary anthropologist David Barash (2016) argues that humans evolved to be polygynous rather than monogamous. He characterizes this evolved structure of human kinship as including one "harem master" and several subordinate females. Despite the brutish and male dominant evolutionary past, Barash argues, humans can rise above nature and establish monogamous marriage as a remedy to the male dominance necessary to maintain polygynous ties. He argues that,

Despite our shared polygamous history and the fact that somewhere deep inside everyone there lurks the ghosts of our harem-holding (for men) and harem-hiding (for women) pasts, by virtue of being human we also have the capacity—*should we choose to do so*—to make conscious, deliberate, mindful choices that refute our polygamously generated inclinations.

(Barash 2016: 203, emphasis added)

Humans are different from every other animal species in that we have a "behavioral repertoire [that] includes cognition, culture, symbolism, language, and so forth. As a result, we are almost certainly less constrained by our biology than any other species" (Barash 2016: 210). If humans are interested in gender equality and a more democratic and free society, Barash concludes, we must codify monogamous marriage the only legitimate form of kinship.

With a poly gaze we realize that, of course, the flip side of this mononormative argument is the lurking, Western, colonial assumption that any culture that still practices polygamy must be less rational, cultured, democratic and still ruled by brutish nature rather than culture. Not unlike the nineteenth-century rhetoric about Mormon polygamy, Barash links polygamy with Arab Muslims by calling dominant men in polgyny "harem masters," and equates monogamy with culture and civility.

Contemporary U.S. discourse about Muslims and citizenship repeat this narrative about polygamy, male dominance, and despotism. Margaret Denike argues that anti-polygamy sentiment

> continues to function through current-yet-archaic criminal laws in Canada and the United States and their selective enforcement, and to inform anti-Chinese and anti-Muslim immigration policy and jurisprudence, where the very possibility of practicing polygamy has long been a condition of exclusion in both states.
>
> *(Denike 2010: 855)*

Similarly to how Mormon women who practice polygamy are cast as brainwashed victims, Muslim women are also assumed to be passive and victimized, especially if they are involved in polygamous marriages (Majeed 2016; Park 2016). Focusing on African American Muslims in particular, Debra Majeed writes,

> Attention to polygyny among African Americans…occurs at a time when Western discourses about Islam concentrate on what are perceived to be the abnormalities of Muslim life, especially after the events of September 11, 2001, and on the agency available to Muslim women to structure their public and private spheres.
>
> *(Majeed 2016, 88)*

Unlike contemporary U.S. constructions of Muslims, explicit arguments about race treason in particular have gone by the wayside in contemporary, mainstream public discourse about the FLDS. However, the conflation of polygamy with despotism and barbaric gender relations continues. For instance, Lori Beaman (2016) compellingly argues that Canada's anti-polygamy laws and a 2010 Supreme Court of British Columbia decision to uphold those laws rely upon the assumption that polygamy is inherently oppressive to women (and children) and polygamist women are passive victims of brainwashing. Based on an analysis of testimonies offered by experts and the final decision of the court, Beaman concludes that women in polygamous marriages were assumed to be, without exception, subordinate and oppressed by their husbands. Because of this false assumption, the court concluded that polygamy is contrary to the interests of the Canadian state to *maintain* gender equality. Beaman argues that the argument and decision relied upon a false presumption that gender equality had been achieved in Canada and that monogamous, heterosexual marriages are inherently equal.

> The argument can be made that even though equality has not been realized, it is an important goal that justifies the criminalization of polygamy. There is no disputing that women's equality is an important goal, but I take issue with the idea that criminalizing a particular family form will further the advancement of women's equality. If this were the case, there is sufficient evidence of women's continuing inequality (unequal division of labor, disadvantages women face in the paid labor force as a result of their inequality in the home, and violence against women in the domestic setting) within monogamous family forms to consider criminalizing it as well.
>
> *(Beaman 2016: 48)*

Beaman goes on to argue that the voices of women who offered affidavits in favor of religious freedom and the practice of polygamy were silenced and the women themselves were dismissed as suffering from false consciousness and thus untrustworthy in the veracity of their testimony.

> In discussions about polygamy, women enter in two related ways: the first is that women (and usually children are mentioned in the same breath to create a "women-and-children" merger) suffer harm in polygamous relationships and need to be protected from them; the second is that polygamy flies in the face of women's equality, and thus modern society and the nation-state must be defended against it…the protection of women becomes equated with the protection of nation. Arguments about women's equality contain the core premise that women's equality has in fact been achieved and that polygamy represents a practice that threatens to undermine that equality.
>
> *(Beaman 2016: 44)*

Based on decades of researching several different religions in North America, Beaman concludes that this is due to a broader

> [Western] framework that has consistently denied agency to some religious women. Women who are religious, especially fundamentalist, orthodox, observant, or practicing (as they are variously labeled and label themselves) are not imagined to make choices in the same way as the 'free' women of the sexually liberated neoliberal market-capitalist world.
>
> *(Beaman 2016: 43)*

Much like the anti-Mormon rhetoric of the nineteenth century, women who choose to enter and remain in polygamous marriages are assumed to be subject to despotic indoctrination while women who enter into monogamous marriages are assumed to be always making free and rational decisions.

Shelley Park (2016) is also critical of how FLDS and polygamous women are constructed through mainstream media and argues that these renderings are not just mononormative; they are also metronormative. Because the FLDS do not subscribe to neo-liberal notions of the good life—urban, monogamous, consumerist—they are, according to Park, a subaltern Other.

> To see the FLDS mother as a subaltern subject...shifts our attention to our *own* role in perpetuating violence against FLDS women and children. When we claim to "know" that all FLDS women and children are held captive by dominating and abusive patriarchs in the rural spaces they inhabit, we practice a form of epistemic imperialism that upholds culturally dominant ideals of western freedoms and progress—ideals, as I have argued, closely linked to urban living and capital accumulation. Against this hegemonic discourse, members of FLDS communities are imagined as primitive or barbaric. A failure to desire what we have and to live how we live is *unimaginable* to us; thus, we infer that the rural Other is either stupid (uneducated, brainwashed) or dangerous (morally degenerate) or both (dangerous because brainwashed).
>
> *(Park 2016: 87)*

Park's research suggests that, in many cases, mainstream media hold FLDS women responsible for allowing men to abuse their children, and, yet, in their coverage rarely talk with or present the perspective of FLDS women or their children. In either case—women are brainwashed victims or complicit—mainstream media commentary is from a deeply Western, middle-class, and urban perspective.

This produces what Park (2016) identifies as "an urban/rural dichotomy" that maps on to the "metropolitan subject (representing the Empire's center)" in opposition to "the primitive and often ignoble savage who dwells outside of the city in isolation from civilizing intellectual, aesthetic and ethical influences" (88). Park goes on to note that "the urban/rural dichotomy crosscuts the monogamy/polygamy dichotomy to brand some North American (rural) polygamists as dangerous while positioning other North American (urban) polygamists as civilized" (Park 2016: 88). Most relatively positive television portrayals of Mormon polygamous families render them acceptable because they embody American ideals for the "metropolitan subject." Park finds that, in shows like *Big Love* and *Sister Wives*, for instance, "suburban polygamists" are tolerable and entertaining as long as they espouse neo-liberal ideology about consumerism, feminism, and the nation-state. Park goes on to define these portrayals of good, suburban polygamists as deeply polynormative.

> The positive reception of suburban polygamy as featured recently on television, in books, on the radio and the internet, illustrates a trend towards

understanding polygamy as a potentially rational kinship choice and a trend towards adjudicating *some* polygamous families (those formed through mutual, rational, consent) as morally acceptable. Being a polygamist is no longer sufficient, on its own, to mark one as an "unfit" (or even a non-feminist) parent. Polynormativity links the acceptability of polygamy as a rational "lifestyle" choice consistent with ethical parenting to iconic symbols of "first world" neoliberal consumption: minivans, smart phones, little league, music lessons, high school and college education, dinner dates, sushi, steak, wine, sprawling suburban homes, family vacations and commuter marriages.

(Park 2016: 80)

As long as contemporary polygamous families look and act like "normal" monogamous *and* polyamorous families (urban, secular, consumerist, gender enlightened, and white—there are no positive portrayals of suburban, Muslim polygamists), they are acceptable.

It is in this socio-historical context where "bad" polygamy is cast as despotic, inherently male dominant, rural, and associated with criminality, child sexual abuse, women's oppression, and barbarism that John Krakauer constructs his narrative in *Under the Banner of Heaven*.

Krakauer's *Under the Banner of Heaven*: A story of mononormative journalism

John Krakauer's book, *Under the Banner of Heaven: A Story of Violent Faith*, is a well-written and researched, page-turning account of the murder of Brenda Lafferty and her 2-year-old daughter, Erica. Their murderers were self-proclaimed polygamists and Brenda's brothers-in-law, Dan and Ron Lafferty. The overarching argument of the book is that after reading *The Peace Maker* (Jacob 1842), a pamphlet that outlines "the principle" or the importance of men's dominance over women, which includes polygamous marriage, the Lafferty brothers became obsessed with polygamy and women's subordination. Brenda Lafferty was strong-willed, educated, and refused to bow down to what Ron Lafferty was advocating. She also encouraged other women in the family to resist. Quoting Brenda's sister Betty, Krakauer (2004) writes, "Brenda was the only one in the Lafferty wives who was educated…and her education was what they were afraid of" (155). Ron Lafferty insisted that women's subservience to men was the will of God, and that, because of her defiance and growing influence on other women in the family, Brenda would be better off dead than damned to hell for eternity.

As the subtitle of the book suggests, Krakauer's focus is on the religious fanaticism of the Lafferty brothers. However, a close poly reading reveals that Krakauer was not just taking on religious fanaticism; he was also taking on polygamy. Because of his own obsession with polygamy, Krakauer is unable to separate religious fanaticism, male dominance, and polygamy. As is often the case in contemporary mainstream media coverage of the FLDS, he ends up spinning a rather mononormative, metronormative, and deeply Western narrative about polygamy, and comes very close to blaming polygamy for the murders rather than male dominance or the individuals who perpetrated the crime.

From the start, Krakauer places polygamy at the center of his narrative by recounting the break between the mainstream LDS and the FLDS over the practice of polygamy as the historical context of the murders. The language Krakauer uses to draw a distinction between the mainstream LDS and the FLDS reflects and perpetuates broader stereotypes of polygamy as a social and cultural problem. Krakauer (2004) describes the break as a positive step for the mainstream LDS: "Having jettisoned polygamy, Mormons gradually ceased to be regarded as a crackpot sect" (7). He goes on to describe how contemporary members of the FLDS are an embarrassment to the mainstream church.

> Mormon authorities treat the fundamentalists as they would a crazy uncle—they try to keep the "polygs" hidden in the attic, safely out of sight, but the fundamentalists always seem to be sneaking out to appear in public at inopportune moments to create unsavory scenes, embarrassing the entire LDS clan...and no aspect...makes the church more defensive than "plural marriage."
>
> *(Krakauer 2004: 6)*

The analogy between "polygs" and a "crazy uncle" who is "hidden in the attic" is more about polygamy than about religious fanaticism, the supposed focus of the book and explanation for the murders.

In the chapter devoted entirely to polygamy, Krakauer argues that polygamy is an especially patriarchal structure for marriage and gender relations.

> Mormonism is a patriarchal religion...Men, and only men, are admitted to the priesthood and given positions of ecclesiastical authority, including that of prophet...All of this holds true in both the mainstream LDS Church and in the Fundamentalist Church, although the fundamentalists take these rigid notions—of obedience, of control, of distinct and unbending roles for men and women—to a much greater extreme. The primary responsibility of women in FLDS communities (even more than in the mainline Mormon culture) is to serve their husbands, conceive as many babies as possible, and raise those children to become obedient members of the religion.
>
> *(Krakauer 2004: 33)*

According to Ertman (2010), however, both mainstream versions of monogamous marriage and the fundamentalist practice of polygamy are grounded in a patriarchal structure. Ertman writes:

> both forms of marriage assigned men and women rights and responsibilities based on their status. Status-based rules excluded monogamous wives from

aspects of public life such as the practice of law. Along the same lines, the "Patriarchal Principle," as the Mormons called polygamy, reaffirmed the status-based authority of fathers and husbands that the rest of America was slowly leaving behind. In short, status and contract played key roles in both monogamy and polygamy.

(Ertman 2010: 291)

Still, Krakauer understates the extent of male dominance in monogamous Mormonism (and fundamentalist Christianity, for that matter) and attributes oppressive gender relations solely to the practice of polygamy.

The Peace Maker offered an elaborate biblical rationale for polygamy in which it proposed as a cure of the myriad ills that plagued monogamous relationships and, by extension, all of humankind. Part of that cure was making sure that women remained properly subservient as God intended.

(Krakauer 2004: 90)

Devoting an entire chapter to "the principle" of polygamous marriage, Krakauer situates the Lafferty brothers' fanaticism squarely in the culture of the FLDS despite the fact that the Laffertys were not members of the FLDS.

Although Dan Lafferty advocated plural marriage at the time of the murders, he did not come from an FLDS family. There is, however, every indication that his family of origin, though unaffiliated with the FLDS, was thoroughly controlled by his extremely cruel and abusive father, Watson Lafferty. Krakauer (2004) describes the Lafferty household by quoting Dan Lafferty.

Dan [Lafferty] characterizes his dad as "strong-willed," a "very individual individual," and "strict about a lot of things." In fact, Watson Lafferty was a formidable disciplinarian who did not hesitate to beat the living tar out of his children and wife, Claudine, to enforce his rules. Commonly, the children were present to witness the punishment when Watson hit Claudine…The children were also present when Watson clubbed the family dog to death with a baseball bat.

Importantly, Watson Lafferty was not a polygamist. "Although Dan's father adhered rigidly to Mormon doctrine, he could not be called a fundamentalist. 'I don't think the word polygamy was ever mentioned while I was growing up,' says Dan. 'It never even crossed my mind'" (91). Despite Dan Lafferty's abusive, patriarchal, and *monogamous* family of origin, Krakauer insists on explaining the murder as a result of Dan Lafferty's adherence to the FLDS covenant of plural marriage. Referring to *The Peacemaker* as a rationale for polygamy, and only secondarily an excuse for women's subordination, Krakauer attributes Ron Lafferty's obsession with Brenda Lafferty to polygamy rather than to his obsession with her education, independence, and willingness to stand up to him.

To make his case and contextualize the murders within polygamy rather than patriarchy, Krakauer spends a great deal of time outlining the various crimes perpetrated against women and girls at the hands of men in the FLDS. For instance, he compares the kidnap and rape of Elizabeth Smart with the forced marriage of Ruby Jessop, a member of the FDLS who was compelled by her family to marry an older, polygamous man.

Elizabeth Smart, a 14-year-old and member of the LDS, was abducted from her bedroom at knifepoint by Brian David Mitchell. Mitchell identified as a Mormon Fundamentalist and abducted Smart in order to make her his second wife, but he was not affiliated with the FLDS. Describing Mitchell's rationale for the abduction, Krakauer (2004) writes, "On Thanksgiving Day 2000, Mitchell announced to Barzee (his wife) and anyone else who would listen that he had received a revelation in which the Lord commanded him to take seven additional wives" (45). As reported by Krakauer, Flora Jessop, a former member of the FLDS and anti-polygamist activist who was forced to marry her cousin at the age of 14, contacted the media in Phoenix to suggest that a polygamist had abducted Elizabeth Smart. "Jessop is extremely relieved that Elizabeth Smart was discovered alive and thinks the outpouring of support Elizabeth has received is wonderful. But in Jessop's view it underscores the disturbing absence of support for another young victim of *polygamy*—her sister" (51, emphasis added). Both Krakauer and, apparently Jessop, perceive the young women as victims, as no doubt they are. However, in Krakauer's reporting in the book, the young women were victims, first and foremost, of polygamy, not male violence and patriarchal indoctrination.

Certainly, in both cases, the girls were forced, one at knifepoint and one with the threat of eternal damnation, to marry older men and were subsequently and repeatedly raped. However, neither case is necessarily about plural marriage per se as much as they are about men using violence and religious doctrine to control, possess, and sexually assault young women. Quoting an "antipolygamy activist" Lorna Craig, Krakauer (2004) writes:

> Craig notes that both Elizabeth and Ruby were fourteen when they were kidnapped, raped, and "kept captive by *polygamous* fanatics." The main difference in the girls' respective ordeals, she says, is that "Elizabeth was brainwashed for nine months," while Ruby had been brainwashed by *polygamous* fanatics "since birth."
>
> *(52, emphasis added)*

Notice that Krakauer (2004) doesn't refer to the perpetrators of these crimes as *religious* fanatics. His and Craig's emphasis is on polygamy, not religion. "[Quoting Craig], 'I would say that teaching a girl that her salvation depends on her having sexual relations with a married man is inherently destructive. Such relationships, Craig argues bitterly, should be considered 'a crime, not a religion'" (53). I couldn't agree more. However, *any* indoctrination, religious or secular, that convinces young women to go along with forced marriage, accept sexual assault as normal, and obey their husbands or face severe consequences is abhorrent. This would be the case in forced monogamous marriage as well. And yet, both Krakauer and Craig conflate the abhorrent crimes of forced marriage and rape with polygamy. As they do so, they assume that polygamy is, by definition, abusive. This assumption, of course, implicitly upholds the deeply American narrative that monogamous marriage is, by comparison, always more egalitarian and purely voluntary.

Krakauer also conflates domestic, physical abuse with polygamy. For instance, discussing the marriage of Ruth Stubbs at the age of 16 to Rodney Holm, a man twice her age and already married to two women, including Ruth's elder sister, Krakauer (2004) states,

> But polygamy is a crime in all fifty states, as well as in Canada, and police officers are sworn to uphold the law. This point became problematic for Chief Roundy…when Ruth Stubbs—the third wife of one of his police officers—fled Colorado City with her two children and appeared on the evening news in Phoenix, complaining that she had been beaten by her husband, Rodney Holm, and that polygamy is intrinsically abusive.
>
> *(27–28)*

Again, there is a mononormative sleight-of-hand here when Krakauer slips from a description of domestic violence as abusive (which it always is) and polygamy as "intrinsically abusive." The conflation of polygamy with domestic violence and abuse masks the prevalence of abuse in monogamous families (Beaman 2016; Bennion 2016a) and implicitly renders monogamous marriages as free from abuse. By equating polygamy with abuse and monogamy with safety, Krakauer perpetuates the dangerous and *false* assumption that polygamy is the problem rather than men's use of violence to maintain dominance and control over women in monogamous and polygamous marriages.

While Krakauer assumes that polygamy is intrinsically abusive to women and children, the research literature on polygamy suggests otherwise. Rather than assume monogamy is free of abuse, and polygamy is always oppressive, empirical researchers who study polygamous families approach this juxtaposition as an empirical question and ask, what are the conditions under which abuse and domestic violence are more or less likely in all families? They find that isolation, male dominance, and men's sole control of resources and authority are conducive to abuse in both monogamous and polygamous families.

Researchers find that the extent of abuse depends on the context and the type of polygamy practiced. For instance, Janet Bennion (2016a) distinguishes between *polygamy*, which simply refers to plural marriage, and *elite polygyny*, a particularly male dominant system in which only a small number of elite men have access to many wives. After conducting a review of the literature on polygamy worldwide, including among FLDS populations, Bennion (2016a) concluded that there are specific conditions associated with "poor-functioning polygyny." They include the criminalization of polygamy, which leads many polygamists, including women who are experiencing abuse, to be fearful of law officials. This makes it impossible for women and children to report abuse. Because of the illegality, many polygamists are socially, geographically, and religiously isolated, and the more isolated a family or sect, the more likely abuse will occur and go unpunished. Bennion also finds in her meta-analysis of research on polygamy that there is significant variance in the extent of inequality between husband and wives and among wives. The more male dominant a family or social structure is, and the extent to which men control all of the valued resources (including women and children), the more likely women and children will experience abuse. Another factor that correlates with abuse is economic deprivation, which leads to overcrowded households and an inequitable distribution of resources to wives. This in turn can lead wives to feel marginalized, and competition inhibits female solidarity and networking (Bennion 2016a: 64–65). In sum, Bennion's survey of the empirical literature on polygamy contradicts mononormative assumptions that monogamy is always good for women and polygamy is always bad. Instead, she finds that both monogamy and polygamy are variable in the extent to which women benefit or are harmed, and variability will depend on context and the conditions under which monogamy or polygamy are lived.

In addition, empirical research demonstrates that mononormative assumptions about the passivity and complicity of polygamous women are also inaccurate. For instance, Bennion (2016b) interviewed polygamous women and found that many women are willing to enter into polygamous marriages and sometimes reap significant benefits. Unmarried women, single mothers, and divorced and widowed women in the mainstream LDS are often socially ostracized and economically disadvantaged. Bennion (2016b) found that, for these women, polygamy is an attractive option, especially if they can find a husband who is able to provide for them and their children. While some women do experience economic deprivation and/or physical, emotional, or sexual abuse within the context of polygyny (as do some women in monogamous marriages), many women describe having positive and mutually caring and supportive relationships with co-wives. Bennion concludes, "While many women find greater access to valued resources and are quite content in polygyny, other women are dissatisfied because of abuse, abandonment, poverty, or co-wife jealousy" (Bennion 2016a: 62–63).

In the case of African American Muslim women who choose to join a polygamous marriage, Majeed (2016) suggests that polygamy can be "one remedy for and a demographic challenge to the absence of marriageable African American men and/or the high number of female-led households" (97). Majeed, like Bennion, resists the impulse to cast polygamous women as brainwashed, passive, and/or forced by barbaric men into polygamy. Instead, she emphasizes the heterogeneity of reasons for and experiences of polygamous marriage.

What it means to live polygyny is often constructed upon divisions along a spectrum that includes women who affirm the practice, those who acquiesce to what they read as a "right" Muslim men have been given by Allah, and those who gladly accept the marginality of polygyny as a site of resistance.

(Majeed 2016: 99)

Finally, in the last 25 years there has been an emergence of what Bennion (2016b) calls "progressive polygamy." These polygynous sects and families explicitly embrace feminism and forge a family structure that is, to be sure, patriarchal in that only men can have more than one spouse, but also one that cultivates women's autonomy, self-actualization, and authority in household matters. For some women, progressive polygamy is an opportunity to form emotionally and sexually intimate relationships with other women without violating church doctrine that prohibits homosexuality and requires heterosexual marriage. In his telling of the Lafferty brothers and their murderous ways, an isolated incident to be sure, Krakauer is either unaware of or chose to ignore the empirical literature that clearly shows variability in how polygamy takes shape and functions in FLDS families.

Conclusion

In a rather scathing review of *Under the Banner of Heaven*, historian and librarian at the LDS Family History Library, Craig Foster (2004) points his criticism squarely in Krakauer's opposition to religion and especially the Church of Latter-Day Saints. Foster (2004) also recognizes that Krakauer is rather fanatical in his opposition to polygamy. "Perhaps Krakauer's most volatile statements appear when he discusses one of the main themes of his book, plural marriage" (169). Foster (2004) questions the historical accuracy of *Under the Banner of Heaven* and, in particular, the way in which Krakauer casts Joseph Smith as a pedophile and child marriage as endemic to the religion. "Beyond being simply offensive, Krakauer's comments are problematic in several ways. First, Joseph Smith did not marry a plurality of fourteen year olds…Second, the idea that Smith married a parcel of pubescent girls is sheer fallacy" (170). Foster continues,

> [Krakauer] demonstrates his own ignorance in regard to historical research and analysis. And, while some errors can be expected from a novice attempting to deal with the Latter-day Saint past, not everything Krakauer has done in his book can be viewed as innocent mistakes. Indeed, with whatever agenda in mind, Krakauer appears to have created a book that focuses on the negative and sensational in order to portray the church in an unflattering light.
>
> *(Foster 2004: 173)*

Foster's review, however, does not take issue with the myth-perpetuating inaccuracies in Krakauer's portrayal of polygamy.

This is not surprising given Foster's extensive commentary on polygamy in LDS history. Foster believes that, in order to surpass associations between Mormonism and polygamy, the LDS must embrace their polygamous ancestors and reject any sense of shame associated with that past. In an article published in *The Interpreter*, a Mormon publication, Foster (2018) draws an analogy between contemporary LDS members and its polygamous past with a difficult marriage, separation, and divorce. He writes,

> When marriages suffer from serious problems, separation almost always leads to either reconciliation with the hopes of the marriage surviving or to divorce. While some periods of separation are longer and uglier than others, a finality is almost always achieved. Unfortunately, such an outcome is not the case for Latter-day Saints and their polygamous history. Since few anticipate plural marriage's return, and even fewer hope for it, the estranged partners are not getting back together...With every separation or divorce comes uncomfortable reminders of former relatives. In many ways, Fundamentalist Mormons are like Latter-day Saints' former relatives—ex-uncles or crazy former cousins who cause embarrassment and discomfort, for they remind us of a married past we would rather forget.
>
> *(Foster 2018: 75)*

While Foster advocates LDS members acknowledging their polygamous ancestors in order to move forward, he, like Krakauer, adopts rather mononormative language by using the analogy of "crazy former cousins." For Foster, polygamy is something in the past, but it is not in the now or future. Mainstream Mormons, he argues, should not be associated with polygamy except in a historical sense. Despite his negative (and accurate) review of *Under the Banner of Heaven*, Foster ironically agrees with Krakauer by suggesting that polygamy constitutes the "negative" and "sensational" parts of the church's past. Foster espouses the same mononormative ideology when, instead of questioning Krakauer's mononormative assumptions, he questions the historical accuracy of Krakauer's characterization of Joseph Smith. It speaks volumes that Foster cannot question the general denigration of polygamy for he must distance himself from the "crazy former cousins." Moreover, and significantly, nowhere does Foster advocate members of the LDS acknowledge the patriarchal and racist past of the LDS in order to surpass women's subordination and white supremacy. Only plural marriage is the source of embarrassment and discomfort, and thus polygamy must be jettisoned to the past.

In his compelling, page-turning story about a horrifying murder, John Krakauer falls into the same trap by blaming polygamy rather than the Lafferty brothers for the murders. As a journalist who clearly conducted extensive research, he provides ample evidence to suggest that the Lafferty brothers, though not embedded within the FLDS, completely embraced the ideology that a devout life can only be led by practicing polygyny. However, Krakauer's own mononormative rejection of plural marriage and adherence to very old colonial narratives about polygamy, lead him to conflate male dominance, men's violence, and women's subordination with polygamy. By blaming polygamy for the murders, he glosses the role of structural gender inequality, geographic isolation, and the criminalization of polygamy as the context in which the Lafferty brothers could adopt the theological doctrine of *The Peacemaker* as a rationale for having control over and sexual access to the women in their lives. This is a subtle, but important point. Krakauer believes and perpetuates the Western myth that polygamy leads to gender inequality, abuse, and despotism. The empirical literature, however, reverses this causal narrative and shows that men as a class can serve their gender interests, such as controlling resources and having authority over women, by using religious doctrine as a legitimating rationale for establishing a decidedly male dominant form of polygyny and force others to go along. The problem is not then, polygamy as a form of marriage. The problem is male dominance and gender inequality, as well as the criminalization of polygamy and geographic isolation, all of which leave women with few options and men with control over resources.

My goal in this chapter was to adopt a poly gaze to highlight how mainstream perceptions of the FLDS and polygamy more generally are deeply mononormative. They presume and articulate the myth that monogamy is superior, more evolved, egalitarian, democratic, and thus, more American than polygamy. This mono-normative narrative about citizenship masks the pervasiveness of abuses and oppression within monogamous, heterosexual marriages while simultaneously legitimating the persecution of religious and ethnic minorities and immigrant populations.

In the nineteenth century, the Mormon polygamous family was rendered degenerative, chaotic, and non-white, and Mormon men were represented as unable to fulfill the role of head of household or head of state. In the wake of the U.S. civil rights movement, feminist women's movements, and the emergence of polyamory as a subculture, the colonial and racial history of anti-polygamy laws and sentiment appears to have been forgotten, but the gender narrative continues. This is especially true for contemporary polyamorists in the United States.

Polyamorists often are quick to state that polyamory is *not* the same thing as polygamy. The sometimes explicit but often unstated rationale for this distinction is that polyamory is secular, urban, and gender egalitarian and thus, the opposite of religious, rural, and gender oppressive Muslim and FLDS polygamy. This juxtaposition is deployed as a normalizing strategy to align the practice of poly-amory with heteronormative, metronormative, and secular definitions of citizenship (Rambukkana 2015; Willey 2016). Polyamorists who deploy FLDS or Muslim polygamy as an abject Other in order to legitimate their own sexual and relationship practices, are doing so within the context of U.S. history and the colonial, classed, raced, and gendered persecution of polygamists. The poly gaze reveals that these discursive strategies are never simply about polyamory and polygamy; they are embedded within and constitutive of a long history of mononormative, white supremacist, and colonial narratives about citizenship, human progress, and race.

Finally, despite my effort here to highlight the mononormative, as well as colonial, patriarchal and white supremacist roots of mainstream discourses about polygamy, I am not advocating for the legalization of plural marriage or folding polygamous marriage into already existing heteronormative definitions of good citizenship. Marriage is a system of inequality that benefits some and not others. Instead, I am compelled by the argument made by legal scholar, Kerry Abrams (2016). She writes,

> Rather than resisting polygamy as a threat to traditional [or egalitarian] marriage or embracing it as a civil rights issue, we instead could use it as an opportunity to reevaluate the law of marriage and its relationship to public benefits and legal parentage.
>
> *(229)*

Abrams suggests that de-criminalizing polygamy would alleviate some of the problems experienced by polygamists, especially women, but it would, like same-sex marriage, hinder rethinking families and households outside of or beyond legal marriage.

> [T]he work that family law *beyond* marriage law is currently doing may be where polyamorous relationships are most likely to be recognized, in part or in full. Instead of arguing about decriminalization—which appears at this point to be constitutionally required—legal reformers should pay closer attention to how partial or full recognition of multiple adult-adult and adult-child relationships would help or hinder the family lives of all people, those who consider themselves polygamists and those who do not.
>
> *(Abrams 2016: 247)*

Mononormative discourse about "bad" polygamists as undeserving, and polynormative narratives about "good" polygamists and polyamorists as deserving the rights of citizenship distract from broader conversations about marriage as a system of privilege and its role in facilitating or inhibiting the interests and well-being of women. These discourses reflect and perpetuate the deeply colonial and racist history and continuing persecution of religious and ethnic minorities in the United States and Canada, and they mask this persecution as the moral and legal protection of women and children, not from male dominance or men's violence, but from polygamy.

References

Abrams, Kerry. 2016. "(Mis) Recognizing Polygamy." In Janet Bennion and Lisa Fishbayn Joffe (Eds), *The Polygamy Question*. Boulder: University Press of Colorado.

Barash, David. 2016. *Out of Eden: The Surprising Consequences of Polygamy*. New York: Oxford University Press.

Beaman, Lori. 2016. "Opposing Polygamy: A Matter of Equality or Patriarchy?" In Janet Bennion and Lisa Fishbayn Joffe (Eds), *The Polygamy Question*. Boulder: University Press of Colorado.

Bennion, Joan. 2016a. "The Variable Impact of Mormon Polygyny on Women and Children." In Janet Bennion and Lisa Fishbayn Joffe (Eds), *The Polygamy Question*. Boulder: University Press of Colorado.

Bennion, Joan. 2016b. "Progressive Polygamy in the Western United States." In Ronald C. Den Otter (Ed), *Beyond Same-Sex Marriage: Perspectives on Marital Possibilities*. London: Lexington Books.

Burgett, Bruce. 2005. "On the Mormon Question: Race, Sex, and Polygamy in the 1850s and the 1990s." *American Quarterly* 57(1): 75–102.

Denike, Margaret. 2010. "The Racialization of White Man's Polygamy." *Hypatia* 25(4): 852–874.

Ertman, Martha. 2010. "Race Treason: The Untold Story of America's Ban on Polygamy." *Columbia Journal of Gender and the Law* 19(2): 287–366.

Evans, Martha Bradley. 2011. "The Past as Prologue: A Comparison of the Short Creek and Eldorado Polygamy Raids." In Stuart A. Wright and James T. Richardson (Eds), *Saints Under Siege: The Texas Raid on the Fundamentalist Latter Day Saints*. New York: New York University Press.

Foster, Craig. 2004. "Doing Violence to Journalistic Integrity." *FARMS Review* 16(1): 149–174.

Foster, Craig. 2018. "More than a Plural Marriage Revelation." *Interpreter: A Journal of Mormon Scripture* 29: 219–226.

Jacob, Udney Hay with Joseph Smith. 1842. *The Peacemaker (Pamphlet)*. Nauvoo, Illinois.

Klesse, Christian. 2018. "Bisexuality, Slippery Slopes, and Multipartner Marriage." *Journal of Bisexuality* 18(1): 35–53.

Krakauer, John. 2004. *Under the Banner of Heaven: A Story of Violent Faith*. New York: Anchor.

Majeed, Debra. 2016. "Ethics of Sisterhood: African American Muslim Women and Poly-gyny." In Janet Bennion and Lisa Fishbayn Joffe (Eds), *The Polygamy Question*. Boulder: University Press of Colorado.

Park, Shelley. 2016. "'When We Handed Out the Crayolas, They Just Stared at Them': Deploying Metronormativity in the War Against FLDS Mothers." *Philosophy in the Contemporary World* 23(1): 71–90.

Rambukkana, Nathan. 2015. *Fraught Intimacies: Non/Monogamy in the Public Sphere*. Vancouver: UBC Press.

Symons, Donald. 1979. *The Evolution of Human Sexuality*. New York: Oxford University Press.

Somerville, Siobhan. 2000. *Queering the Color Line: Race and the Invention of Homosexuality in American Culture*. Durham, NC: Duke University Press.

Song, Sarah. 2016. "Polygamy in Nineteenth Century America." In Janet Bennion and Lisa Fishbayn Joffe (Eds), *The Polygamy Question*. Boulder: University Press of Colorado.

Willey, Angela. 2016. *Undoing Monogamy: The Politics of Science and the Possibilities of Biology*. Durham, NC: Duke University Press.

Wright, Stuart and James Richardson. 2011. "Introduction." *Saints Under Siege: The Texas Raid on the Fundamentalist Latter Day Saints*. New York: New York University Press.

3

CASUAL SEX ON CAMPUS

The mononormative narratives told about sexual relationships in heterosexual hookup cultures

The 2018 HBO documentary *Swiped: Hooking Up in the Digital Age* (Sales 2018) is a cautionary tale about how dating apps and social media are transforming the way young people meet potential dating partners. It begins with a young, white woman looking confidently into the camera and describing her uses of social media. With a coy smile and an unapologetic snicker, she confesses that social media makes it easy for her to flirt with men behind her boyfriend's back. She says,

> I am in a committed relationship with a man I love and I really…love him but there are times when I see him snapping girls he's not supposed to or being on Tinder on the third page of his phone…He tells me to move past it…but I'm going to do the same thing.

This first clip cautions that some people use social media to cheat; a theme that runs throughout the documentary. For instance, in another scene, one African American woman wipes away tears as she describes a man she met on social media and really "fell for." After some time, however, she found out that he "had a whole relationship, and [she] didn't know." She concludes that this is a certain type of man.

> The dude who has his girl in half of his photos and his girl is like his everything like I love this woman. Very passionate. Very romantic. And he'll be the first person in your [direct messages] asking you to come to his house at an ungodly hour trying to smoke you up, buy you drinks, have sex with you while his girlfriend's stuff is all over his apartment. But he's all over social media.

While these clips present cheating as the initial dark side of dating apps, the documentary gradually moves into a coherent narrative about how dating apps inhibit the forming of healthy romantic or sexual partnerships. Near the beginning of the film, for example, we meet a white man who explains how dating apps opened up so many possibilities for hooking up with women that he couldn't imagine settling down into a relationship. Later, he meets a woman on Tinder who ends up becoming his live-in girlfriend. The woman explains to the camera, "He was sleeping with five girls a week on Tinder." Adoringly, he asks her, "Then what?" She smiles and confidently says, "And then he met me."

The film then features them using dating apps together to find women with whom they could have threesomes. The man explains, "[She] is what you'd call heteroflexible. So given that, we've been experimenting with having a third. There's not some sort of constraint or restriction on the relationship." She adds, "Also it's fun because we get to play with Tinder again." We then hear the film-maker ask from behind the camera, "So you guys swipe together now on Tinder?" The man replies,

> The generation before, you meet someone in your hometown. You date them. They're like your high school sweetheart. You date them and that's really the only person you've been with and that kind of monogamy is super scary. And [they] go on for like 60 years in a vanilla type of existence, and it's super bland, and then you die. So, praising the whole swiping fad that's going on right now, [it] introduces you to people you never would have crossed paths with.

Then the woman looks at him and asks, "Could we see each other doing this forever? I don't know." He says, "I mean, definitely not past 60." Shocked, she says, "Not past 60! I was thinking not past…I'm 27 so not past 30!" Resigned, he looks at the camera and says, "Oh, okay." This scene sets up the last segment in the documentary in which we find out that the couple has broken up. In the post-breakup interview, the woman says to her former partner, "You used to be like, four or five times a day, I'm going to marry you. Remember that?" Looking at the camera he says, "I could have been delusional. I mean it felt right at the time." Appearing a bit embarrassed by his response, she says, again to the camera, "He was excited about having someone to love. There's nothing wrong with that." Back-pedaling, he explains, "All I wanted to do is say let's be friends but keep it open ended." Clearly, according to the sequencing of interviews and how this couple is portrayed, dating apps inhibit healthy, long-lasting relationships, as evidenced by their non-monogamous search for a third and their eventual break up.

As we meet the queer and straight, racially and geographically diverse group of 20-somethings struggling to find their way through the new world of on-line flirtation and hooking up, a host of experts including evolutionary biologists, sexologists, dating app techs, and the founders of Tinder and Bumble paint a rather dismal picture of the likelihood of finding a long-term, monogamous relationship through dating apps. For instance, Justin Garcia, a research scientist at the Kinsey Institute and an evolutionary biologist describes "two major transitions since the evolution of social monogamy." The first is the commercialization of dating in the 1950s when dating was moved to public spaces of consumption. The second is the contemporary, digital era in which dating apps are creating in young people a "short-term dating psychology." Garcia avers that, with dating apps, another, potentially more attractive partner is just a swipe away, so young people, especially heterosexual men, are relying exclusively on physical attractiveness and are not taking the time and energy needed to get to know each other. Other experts discuss how this new form of hooking up through dating apps is particularly disadvantageous to women because standards of attractiveness are narrower and harder to achieve for (presumably straight) women. A short-term dating psychology, Garcia argues, makes long-term partnering difficult, if not impossible. This is particularly concerning because we don't know what effect it is having in evolutionary terms. Garcia worries that something else—something more pernicious, will evolve to replace monogamous coupling. Whether or not monogamy is natural or desirable is never discussed, let alone debated.

Dating apps, the film argues, reflect and perpetuate gender inequality and, in the end, make straight women particularly vulnerable to everything from "bad" or unfulfilling sex to being "used," exploited, sexually assaulted, and murdered by predatory men. The problem, the experts in the film tell us, is that dating apps create a hookup culture in which men get their need for sexual novelty fulfilled, and women lose out because they cannot find meaningful and respectful relationships. In another scene, for instance, three white women hang out in a park together and discuss dating and dating apps. One of the women laments,

> I've always wanted that super cute romantic thing where I'm at a book store and a super cute stranger bumps into me…and we have a sweet simple exchange and then we part ways and we come back together later. I feel like that doesn't really happen anymore.

Like this young woman, most of the straight women and queer 20-something cast express dismay and dissatisfaction with the sexual culture in which they find themselves. Meanwhile, the straight men in the film are depicted as enjoying themselves as they describe anonymous hookups as fun, exciting, and above all else, easy. The film is a narrative about the role of dating apps in perpetuating hookup culture and gender inequality, and the straightforward message is that "casual hookups" benefit straight men and are disadvantageous to everyone else.

The filmmaker attempts to hold the creators and purveyors of Tinder and Bumble responsible for this state of affairs by asking them about the likelihood of finding meaningful relationships by swiping. On-screen statistics indicate that 80 percent of Tinder users are looking for long-term relationships, but 81 percent report never having found partners by using a swiping app. The statistics are juxtaposed with Jessica Carbino, a sociologist employed by Tinder, defensively asserting that she has heard otherwise. She asserts, "People say they met and are now living together." Parroting what she has supposedly heard from many Tinder users, she says, "I met the man I'm going to marry. We met on Tinder a year ago and now we're having a baby." The CEO of Tinder claims to know people who "meet on Tinder and get married."

The young straight women and queer people, however, are skeptical. One African American woman says, "Older people in their fifties and sixties don't know what it's like to date now…of course we want to get married and have kids and stuff, but it's not that easy. You can't get yourself pregnant and marry yourself." In a group discussion, this young woman's mother expresses deep concern over these changes in dating culture. She says that when she was dating, "Guys wanted to date you. They weren't like I want to date you, you, and you." Another young woman in the group describes the difference between a "situationship" and a committed relationship. "When people are together and…I don't want to say they're committed. They're sleeping with each other only. They act like they're dating each other but they're not boyfriend and girlfriend. They're not dating. To me that's friends with benefits." Confused, the mother chimes in, "Wouldn't it be a commitment if you guys are exclusive?" Another young woman states unequivocally, "I want a boyfriend. I don't want a fuck buddy." The mother asks, "What does that mean?" The young woman replies, "It means being treated well." Just as there is no discussion of whether or not monogamy is desirable, there is no critical perspective on monogamous marriage as a goal or a measure of relationship success.

By the end of the film, the combination of the expert commentary and the young people's testimony cautions viewers about the dangers of dating apps, but it also tells a story about non-monogamy and "natural" gender differences. Specifically, we're left with the message that men desire sexual novelty without responsibilities or emotional commitment and women desire romance and committed monogamy. Dating apps, the film suggests, benefit men and reflect their interests because dating apps and social media tip the scale toward non-monogamous hookup culture and away from monogamous coupling. The cast of characters, the expert testimony, and the narrative arch of the film do not simply describe gender differences; *they articulate them.*

I begin this chapter with a brief summary of this documentary because the story told through the cast of young people and experts is about the dangers of dating apps (including cheating on a partner, sexual assault, and murder) but, at the same time, and in service to the warnings, the documentary tells a scary tale about hookup culture. The subtext is an all-too-familiar narrative about the difficulties young people face as they desperately pursue meaningful, intimate, and committed relationships. It is familiar because, as I will describe below, decades of social science research suggest that the picture of hookup culture painted by the film is accurate in many ways. High-status straight white men seem to reap most of the benefits of hookup culture, and most everyone else is left dissatisfied, disempowered, and in some cases, traumatized.

However, at the same time, as they describe hookup culture, both the film and the empirical literature tell a similar and familiar story about what constitutes "real" relationships and about gender difference. Both the film and research on hookup culture consistently equate "relationship" with monogamy on the one hand, and non-monogamy with "no-strings-attached" on the other. Stated another way, both the empirical literature and the documentary are *mononormative* in that they implicitly assume *and convey* that 1) monogamous coupling is the optimal way for young people to build fulfilling, emotionally and sexually intimate relationships with other people, and 2) that non-monogamous sexual relations perpetuate gender inequality and put heterosexual women at risk of emotional and/or physical harm.

In this chapter, I adopt a poly gaze to analyze the way in which participants and researchers talk about relationships, hooking up, and gender in hookup culture. I highlight how the participants' responses as they are reported by researchers and, in their analyses of these responses, the researchers themselves assume and reiterate many of the mononormative assumptions circulating in hookup culture. I focus on three academic books and several journal articles *as text* to unpack the stories they tell about the "poly" features of hookup culture. What we'll find is that, while hookup culture makes non-monogamy compulsory, it is driven by deeply mononormative ideas about relationships and gender, and researchers often reproduce these assumptions in their research instruments and reports. Furthermore, as researchers and participants in hookup culture equate relationship with monogamy, they mask the *power* interests of straight, mostly white men and perpetuate essentialist notions of gender difference. A poly rather than mono epistemic lens shows that, by braiding a cautionary tale about the compulsory non-monogamy in hookup culture with a gender narrative about men's desire for sexual freedom and women's desire for relationships, the academic stories we tell about the "poly" norms for hooking up are both mononormative and articulate the very myths about gender differences that serve the interests of straight, white men and are disadvantageous to everyone else.

Gender and power in heterosexual campus hookup cultures

Many university campuses in the United States are characterized by what college students and social science researchers refer to as "hookup culture," a sexual culture in which "casual" sexual interactions between women and men have replaced dating (Bogle 2008; Bradshaw, Kahn, and Saville 2010; England and Thomas 2006; England, Shafer, and Fogarty 2007; Fielder, Carey, and Carey 2012; Manning, Longmore, and Giordono 2006). A substantial sociological and social psychological research literature on heterosexual hooking up has emerged and suggests that there are consistent features of hookup culture that systematically benefit straight white men and work to the disadvantage of women (Armstrong, Hamilton, and England 2010; Heldman and Wade 2010; Kelly 2012; Wade 2017; Wade and Heldman

2012). For instance, some studies show that there is a double standard by which women are judged negatively for hooking up "too much" so many women modify their participation (Bogle 2008; Hamilton and Armstrong 2009; Reid, Elliott, and Webber 2011). Meanwhile men's status is often enhanced through multiple hookups (Fielder and Carey 2010; Gilmartin 2007; Kreager and Staff 2009). Also, men are assumed to be, or report being, interested in hooking up strictly for sexual gratification while women are assumed to be, or report being, interested in developing relationships through hooking up (Bogle 2008). While some women say that they feel empowered by "casual" sex, they also tend to focus on their partner's pleasure instead of their own and engage in undesired behaviors during these sexual encounters (Armstrong, England, and Fogarty 2012; Armstrong, Hamilton, and England 2010; Backstrom, Armstrong, and Puentes 2012; Eshbaugh and Gute 2008; Hamilton and Armstrong 2009; Wade and Heldman 2012). Men are more likely than women to have orgasms during a hookup encounter (Armstrong, England, and Fogarty 2012) and report higher levels of sexual satisfaction and well being after a casual hookup (Bogle 2008; Bradshaw, Kahn, and Saville 2010; Fielder and Carey 2010; Regnerus and Uecker 2011). Related, some men believe that their partners' sexual satisfaction is unimportant in hookups, but most think that it is important in relationships (Armstrong, England, and Fogarty 2012; Backstrom, Armstrong, and Puentes 2012; Kimmel 2008). Women and men research participants report that, unlike in "casual" hookups, within the context of ongoing relationships, women are entitled to sexual pleasure and men have some responsibility for facilitating it (Armstrong, England and Fogarty 2012; Backstrom, Armstrong, and Puentes 2012). The rate of orgasm for women increases when they engage in multiple hookups with the same partner, and the gender gap in orgasm is smallest within the context of what researchers call "committed" or "romantic" relationships compared to "one and done" hookups (Armstrong, England, and Fogarty 2012).

Given this body of research, many researchers conclude that straight men benefit from hookup culture in ways that work against straight women's interests. The main explanations for men's advantage include a skewed gender ratio where women outnumber men, a double standard that makes hooking up costly to women, and men's and women's differing goals in terms of relationships. With a skewed gender ratio, researchers surmise that men have more choices when it comes to partners, and so it is necessary for women to cater to men's needs more than men to women's. Also, when it comes to hookup outcomes, because women want "more" than men—meaning "romantic" or "committed" relationships— interpersonal power dynamics work to men's advantage. In sum, researchers conclude that hookup culture reflects a move away from traditional dating scripts; however, like traditional dating, sex on campuses continues to be structured by hetero-masculine privilege and control.

While this large and growing body of research provides a clear and consistent picture of how gender differences structure the experience of, attitudes toward, and consequences of hooking up, and the explanations for these differences are compelling, there is a rather significant structuring feature of hookup culture, namely *mononormativity*, which remains under-theorized and under-researched in the empirical literature.

Mononormativity refers to institutionalized rituals, customs, narratives, and practices that establish the monogamous couple as the only legitimate and moral structure for emotionally and sexually intimate relationships (Pieper and Bauer 2005). Mononormativity includes a set of widely shared assumptions that all "real" relationships are monogamous and that everyone will eventually settle into a monogamous couple relationship in adulthood. According to a mono(normative) rather than poly view of relationships, dyadic monogamy is synonymous with emotional intimacy, commitment, and romance, and the benefits and satisfactions that come with long-term, committed and intimate relationships are assumed to be only possible within the context of monogamous coupling. From a poly perspective, in contrast, sexual exclusivity between two people is neither necessary nor sufficient for establishing a caring, emotionally intimate relationship in which partners are mutually responsible for each other's well-being. In other words, a poly view of the world rejects compulsory monogamy.

Compulsory monogamy refers to the social arrangements that push individuals toward monogamous coupling as an indicator of and inevitable component of adult responsibility and maturity (Mint 2004). One of the main mechanisms of compulsory monogamy is the erasure of consensual and ethical non-monogamy as a viable and legitimate relationship strategy within the context of "romantic," "serious," or "committed" relationships. In a mononormative world characterized by compulsory monogamy, "serious" relationships are, by definition, monogamous and, to the extent that emotional responsibility and accountability are expected only within the context of "serious" relationships, it is assumed that there should be no expectations for interpersonal responsibility and accountability in "casual," non-monogamous relationships. In a poly world where compulsory monogamy is rejected, emotional responsibility and accountability are expected in all relationships, including non-monogamous ones. A poly gaze opens up a view from which we can identify the workings of mononormativity in how we talk or write about relationships, including in the empirical, academic writings about American hookup culture.

Mononormativity in the (academic) stories we tell about hookup culture

Hookup culture on college campuses and the empirical research on the gender dynamics of hooking up are mononormative in that college students *and* researchers assume that "relationships" are sexually exclusive. This is significant because, as I will show below, mononormative definitions of relationships are central to and secure men's advantage in hookup culture. In other words, mononormativity, compulsory monogamy, and assumptions about "real" relationships circulating in heterosexual hookup cultures set up and legitimate the very real gender dynamics and outcomes of hooking up on college campuses.

Though it may seem surprising or counter-intuitive that mononormativity and compulsory monogamy are central organizing features of the explicitly and compulsively *non-monogamous* hookup culture, hooking up is defined by and intelligible through its difference from sexually exclusive, long-term, couple relationships. Both college students and researchers assume that, when it comes to being sexually active, forming a "serious," meaning *monogamous*, relationship with one person is the only alternative to "casually" hooking up. In this equation, monogamy is synonymous with "relationships," non-monogamy is synonymous with "casual" hook ups, and, therefore, "relationships" and non-monogamy are contradictory and incompatible strategies for sexual intimacy.[1] One result is that any notion of consensual non-monogamy within the context of relationships is rendered invisible. Moreover, the conflation of monogamy with relationships translates into the assumption that relationship *ethics and responsibilities* like open communication, mutual sexual satisfaction, and gender egalitarianism are only relevant within the context of sexual exclusivity. In other words, mononormativity leaves college students with no way of thinking about or demanding relationship ethics and responsibilities in the context of the non-monogamous sexual culture of hooking up.

This lack of a set of agreed upon ethics and responsibilities within the context of non-monogamous relationships is a central organizing feature of the gender structure of heterosexual hookup culture and, as such, systematically works to the advantage of straight men. It does so because perceived and real gender differences in hooking up result from, not just skewed gender ratios, the double standard, and women's and men's differing goals, but also and significantly the inability of college students to imagine and forge *caring and consensual non-monogamous relationships*. Moreover, not only is mononormativity central to the social organization of hookup culture, compulsory monogamy undergirds and legitimates the *effects* of skewed gender ratios, the double standard, differing goals for women and men, and on the resulting power dynamics, experiences, and outcomes of hooking up.

In one of the first academic books on hookup culture, *Hooking Up: Sex, Dating, and Relationships on Campus*, Kathleen Bogle (2008) provides compelling data that the women in her sample consistently conflate the label "relationship" with sexual exclusivity. For instance, women participants, as quoted by Bogle, say that they know when a hookup partner is no longer interested in hooking up or pursuing an on-going relationship with them when he is seen with another woman.

JEN: You'll hook up with them for a week or two weeks consecutively and then something weird happens [laughing].
KB: Like what?
JEN: Like *you'll see them with [another] girl* one night and you are just standing there. I've seen that happen to my friends. No one ever really…sits you down and says: "I don't think this is working out" [they don't handle it] in a mature way. [Laughing]

(Bogle 2008: 41, emphasis added)

KB: When do you figure out that you're not really together?

REBECCA: Umm, *when there's another girl.*

(Bogle 2008: 43, emphasis added)

KB: What about the…word, I think you mentioned it—"talking." If someone says "we're talking" what does that mean?

LANNETTE: It means like, I guess, um, when you're interested in someone, I guess you want to, if you don't already know them you know you want to get to know them so you know you're I guess "talking" to get to know the person… .If you already do know them, like if…you're friends for a while and you start talking—it's more like: "Okay I realize that I might want to be with you." So you spend more time with them and *you kind of limit talking to other guys or girls.*

(Bogle 2008: 67, emphasis added)

"Jen" interprets seeing a hookup partner with another woman as an indication that it's not "working out." Rebecca knows that she and her hookup partners are no longer "together" when there is "another girl." Lanette says that if two people want to "be with" each other, they need to "limit talking to other guys or girls." These are just three examples of what most women in Bogle's sample said: You know you are *not* in a relationship when you see him with another woman. From a mono perspective, the problem is non-monogamy. Namely, the men are seen with other women, which means they are not sexually exclusive, which means there never was a relationship or the relationship is over. This mononormative assumption forecloses open communication about the parameters or meaning of their sexual relationships. While mononormative hookup norms prohibit women from demanding communication outside of the context of a "real" (read monogamous) relationship, men can simply be seen with another woman instead of talking with their hookup partners.

While Bogle identifies the lack of communication as part of the gender power dynamics, she does not, in any portion of the book, identify, let alone discuss, the underlying mononormativity in the participants' reasoning. From a poly perspective, seeing a hookup partner with another person does not foreclose the possibility for communication or continuing a relationship. Communication about expectations would be necessary, *despite* a partner hooking up with others. Unfortunately, this possibility remains invisible in Bogle's interactions with her research participants and in her interpretation of the data.

This is significant because not communicating sets up uneven power dynamics between men and women. For instance, women and men in Bogle's sample also assume that women desire relationships more than men and men's aversion to relationships stems from a stronger desire for sex.

LYNN: If the girl likes the guy, I think she might be interested in finding out if he wants to pursue a relationship. I kind of think guys have this theory that either you hook up or you get married. Like if I was to tell [a guy] I liked him then he would get like so scared and freaked out because [men think]: "Oh my God that means we have to be in a relationship" and it doesn't mean that. I think most girls are looking to try and pursue a relationship, but aren't just going to go up to a guy and be like: "Oh, want to be my boyfriend?" you know what I mean? I think that girls do look for relationships more than guys would.

(Bogle 2008: 80)

KB: Do you have any sense of what people are looking for out of [a hookup]? Do you think people are looking for relationships or the physical...aspects?
GLORIA: I think guys definitely look for the hottest girl and want to "get ass" from that girl and want to say they got it from that girl.

(Bogle 2008: 80)

KB: If someone is not in a relationship, how many times might someone hook up in a semester, like how many different people in a semester?
MARIE: Guys, God, they'll hook up with anybody [laughing], it really just doesn't matter. I've seen guys with a different girl every week; they don't care. I've seen guys cheat on their girlfriends and not care. Girls definitely care more. And I think if girls, even if they're not in a relationship with somebody, but they have hooked up with somebody a couple times, they tend to not hook up with someone else just because they like this person. I think guys will hook up with every other [available] person [even] if they are [primarily] hooking up with one person [laughing].

(Bogle 2008: 80)

Lynn says that men have a "theory" that if women express an emotional component to their relationship, even as tepid as "like," a man will assume his hookup partner wants to marry him. This makes him "freak out" and think that she wants a "relationship." While Lynn is making assumptions about men and what they think, she seamlessly moves from suggesting men's assumptions are unrealistic (e.g. women don't necessarily want marriage) to stating that women do want relationships more than men.

Many women quoted in Bogle's book also assume that men's desire for sex with different women is incompatible with, and excuses them from "caring" or treating, hookup partners well. In Marie's statement above, for instance, she conflates "caring" and a desire for exclusivity on the part of women and collapses "not caring" into a desire for sex. This, too, is a consistent pattern across the quotes Bogle provides.

REBECCA: I think girls…go to parties where they think the same guy [they have hooked up with before] is going to be. I think they try to hook up with the same person. And guys they might [try to hook up with the same person], but I really…don't think so. I think [men's motto is]: the more [girls], the better.

KB: The more different girls, the better?

REBECCA: Yeah, they like to have their little tally kind of thing [laughs]. But, I think most girls want to try to find [or] stick with one guy so they can pretend they're dating them.

KB: What do you mean by that, "pretend they're dating"?

REBECCA: Well, I do it all the time, I haven't had a boyfriend yet, but I had two fake boyfriends. [Laughing] Oh, they were great relationships [sarcastic tone]. *You can kind of think that you're together because you think you're the only one in his life and he seems to care about you, you know?…*You can kind of just make believe that [you're together], like whatever he says you can twist it around to make it seem like something else. So like: "Yes, he loves me [sarcastic tone]!" And all of your friends are telling you that he loves you and that you are bound to be married, but you're never [truly] together. So, it's kind of that whole fake relationship thing.

(Bogle 2008: 43, emphasis added)

Rebecca's "fake" relationship is one in which she imagines that he "cares" for her and that she's "the only one in his life." Men, on the other hand, don't "care," because they feel "the more girls, the better."

MARIE: Because I trusted guys so much…so when I…hooked up, and when they weren't all like lovey-dovey and then I don't know, then I'd hook up with somebody else and I just learned through experience that not every guy is going to fall all over you and be like: "Now I want a girlfriend." You know what I mean? A lot of them just want to hook up with you and then never talk to you again (laughing)…and they don't care!

(Bogle 2008: 43)

Marie equates men being "lovey-dovey" or "fall(ing) all over you" with "caring" and "caring" with being in a girlfriend/boyfriend relationship. When men do not act that way, it is because they "just want to hook up with you and then never talk to you again." Just as women's desire for being treated well by their sexual partners is conflated with a desire for "committed," sexually exclusive relationships, men's interests in avoiding emotional labor and interpersonal responsibility is interpreted as a desire for sex with many different women. The assumption that men's maltreatment of hookup partners stems from a "natural" desire for non-monogamy leaves no room for women to demand anything different, let alone see it as a mechanism of power and control. Marie implicitly assumes that when men don't talk to her after a hookup, it reflects their desire to hookup with others, and because of that desire, she should not expect them to treat her well. This becomes clear when she says, most of the girls I know are looking for *something,* you know someone, even if it's not serious, someone that is there to hang out with and talk to, [girls want] a feeling of being close to someone and I don't know if it's even guys don't want that, it's just they don't care if they have that, it's like: "What-ever." It could be any other girl any night and you know that's fine with them.

(Bogle 2008: 43, emphasis in original)

As Marie so aptly states, women want to "hang out with" and "talk to" and feel "close to someone," not necessarily within the context of a "serious" relationship. Men in Bogle's study make the same false equivalencies between desire for "relationships" and monogamy on the one hand, and aversion to relationships and a desire for sex on the other. As one respondent, Kevin, said, "My attitude is that there are so many girls out there it does not even matter [which one you go after for a hookup]. You can't go psycho over girls, there are just too many of them out there" (Bogle 2008: 56).

Moreover, the discursive conflation of monogamy with treating each other well and non-monogamy with no (emotional or interpersonal) strings masks straight men's power interests. For instance, when women interpret men's maltreatment of them as an indication of men's desire for sex and non-monogamy, they miss the ways in which men's treatment of women relieves men of emotional labor with sexual partners and works to their advantage in terms of power. To the extent that men are expected to "care" and treat women well only in monogamous relationships, men have a vested interest in avoiding relationships, not just because it curtails their ability to hookup with many different women, but also because relationships require emotional labor, interpersonal responsibility, and more egalitarian power dynamics. When men avoid or mistreat their hookup partners, they are interpreted by their hookup partners as wanting non-monogamy rather than avoiding emotional labor. Similarly, when women express a desire for a "caring" partner, this is interpreted as a desire for monogamy rather than a desire for open communication and respect.

As an ideological and central organizing feature of campus hookup cultures, it should come as no surprise that mononormativity shapes, not just assumptions about gender differences in needs and interests, but also the real interests of men and women. If caring treatment, orgasms, and respect are limited to monogamous relationships, women's desire to avoid a reputation and have good sex and caring treatment within the context of egalitarian relationships would, for many of them, manifest as a real desire for a monogamous relationship with one man. Similarly, if men's interests lie in avoiding interpersonal responsibility and emotional labor and having a power advantage over women, it is in their interest to avoid "relationships." The conflation of relationships with monogamy and hookups with no strings attached punctuates gender differences as natural and inevitable (women want relationships/men want sex) while masking the gender *interests* operating—namely that neither men nor women want long-term, committed, and monogamous relationships *and* that women want to be treated well and men want to avoid emotional labor.

While Bogle's analysis of these data is spot on in revealing the *gender assumptions* circulating in hookup culture, she does not unpack how assumptions about mono-gamy, relationships, and hooking are structuring those assumptions and supporting the dynamics. For instance, throughout the book, Bogle (2008), as the interviewer, conflates relationships, sexual exclusivity, and interpersonal responsibility.

The students I spoke with often referred to women initiating "the talk" with men (i.e., a conversation to try to turn a hookup partner into a *boyfriend*). This was one way for women to try to gain control in the hookup scene, which is so fraught with pitfalls for them. Adrienne, a senior at Faith University, had this to say about "the talk":

KB: So were you [and your current boyfriend] considered *exclusive* at some particular point? When did things transition to that?

ADRIENNE: I'd say…we don't really have an anniversary. We don't really subscribe to that, either. But like, um, I made it mid-June. That's when I have my own personal [anniversary] just to keep track. [Laughs] So, about mid-June going into junior year.

KB: So what changed in June?

ADRIENNE: Um, basically I'd come up [to visit him during the summer and] we had like a really fun time and I really liked him and he acted like he liked me. But he's always like, he kind of did this like pull away thing…. But, I was like: "Look I'm really, I'm really starting to like you and I really just don't want to get hurt. Like you tell me yes or you tell me no." He's like: "Oh, of course, you know, I really like you." And then we kind of made it I guess official. So then I started, I kept coming up on the weekends [to visit him over the summer break]…. So we hung out.

(Bogle 2008: 115–116, emphasis added)

In the set up for presenting her data, Bogle defines "the talk" as a "conversation to try to turn a hookup partner into a boyfriend." Then, in her question to Adri-enne, Bogle conflates "boyfriend" with being "exclusive." Not only does Bogle assume this equivalency, she *conveys it* to Adrienne, and, more important, to her readers in the phrasing of her question and interpretation of her data. Even after Bogle conflates "exclusivity" and "boyfriend" in her question, Adrienne does not say anything about having a "talk" about exclusivity. Instead, the "talk" was about how much they like each other, whether or not to spend time together on the weekends, and expectations for on-going connection. In her analysis of this response, Bogle ignores or does not recognize that Adrienne never mentions monogamy or sexual exclusivity. Bogle, in other words, is making the mono-normative assumption many young women and men make—that "relationship" is synonymous with sexual exclusivity. Because of Bogle's own mononormative assumptions, she is unable to analytically separate women's desire for interpersonal communication, responsibility, and accountability on the one hand and a desire for a monogamous relationship on the other.

The mononormative assumption that all "relationships" are sexually exclusive is common, if not ubiquitous (with a couple of exceptions, as I discuss below) in the research on hookup culture. Throughout the empirical literature, researchers use words like "committed," "romantic," or "serious" to distinguish relationships from hookups. While they go to great lengths to define "hooking up" to their participants and their readers, researchers rarely explicitly define what they mean by "committed," "romantic," or "serious." Quite often the implicit meaning of these labels becomes clear when the word "monogamous" or the phrase "sexually exclusive" is slipped in. For instance, in their thorough review of the research literature on hooking up, Heldman and Wade (2010) write, "In the literature, hookup culture is defined as casual sexual contact between *nondating* partners without an (expressed or acknowledged) expectation of forming a *committed relationship*" (324, emphasis added). Two pages later, they write, "While very few hook ups actually lead to a *dating relationship*...students do form committed, *monogamous* relationships [that] evolve out of a string of hook ups" (326, emphasis added). They seamlessly render "committed" and "monogamous" as synonymous and implicitly portray "committed" (monogamy) as the only alternative to "casual" hookups. This slippage between "committed relationships" and monogamy reinforces the idea that "casual" means non-monogamous, and non-monogamy means "no strings attached" in terms of interpersonal responsibility and accountability.

Similarly, Epstein *et al.* (2009) asked college men about their "general level of experience with sexual relationships," by selecting among three choices: "(a) None, very little just starting out; (b) one or two romantic relationships; (c) several romantic relationships" (416). They provide no operational definition for "romantic" nor are there any indications that the meaning of "romantic" was explained to the participants. However, Epstein *et al.* (2009) analyze the responses as if "romantic" and "hooking up" are mutually exclusive, if not opposite. In one figure, they juxtapose the formal hookup script as "No formal or romantic commitment to each other" and provide the example of one respondent saying, "you're not dating." This is juxtaposed to an "alternate script," which is evidenced by a respondent saying, "Oddly enough, I think it would be *monogamous*" (418, emphasis added). By including the quote about monogamy as representative of romantic relationships, Epstein *et al.* (2009) conflate "romantic" and monogamy. When this is contrasted to casual hookups as if non-monogamy and relationships are mutually exclusive, the researchers reinforce the idea that monogamous relationships are equivalent to and always include romantic or caring feelings, and non-monogamy does not. Similarly, Mongeau *et al.* (2013) studied "friends with benefits" relationships, which they define as friends "who are not in a *romantic* relationship, engage in multiple sexual interactions without the expectation that those interactions reflect *romantic* intents or motivations" (38, emphasis added). Like the other researchers, they provide no definition of what a "romantic" relationship is, but they reveal the underlying mononormative definition of "romantic" when they write, "Ideally, FWBRs are simple: "Friends have sex repeatedly with 'no string attached'…the absence of strings suggest a lack of romantic ties, motivations, or expectations *that restrict extra-dyadic behavior*" (Mongeau *et al.* 2013: 38, emphasis added) Further, the instrument administered to participants to distinguish and define friends with benefits relationships (FWBRs) includes the following: FWBR's "involve platonic friends (i.e., those not involved in a romantic relationship) who engage in some degree of sexual intimacy on multiple occasions. This sexual activity could range from kissing to sexual intercourse and is a repeated part of your friendship such that it is not just a one-night stand" (39). Not only does this assume that the meaning of "romantic" is transparent and not in need of definition, the question itself reinforces the idea that "romantic" relationships are juxtaposed with "platonic" ones, another vague term, and then distinguished from "one night stands." They then conclude, "In these data, FWBRs are frequently juxtaposed [by participants] with romantic relationships" (40). Because Mongeau *et al.* (2013) never define "romantic" nor do they ask the participants to provide their own definitions, we have no way of understanding what, exactly, "romantic" means. However, given their typology (Romantic relationships vs. platonic FWBRs vs. one-night-stands), "romantic" really means monogamous (no extra-dyadic behavior), "platonic" means non-monogamous relationship, and one-night stands mean no relationship at all. Because they implicitly define "romantic" as distinct from FWBRs and hooking up, they, like most researchers, reinforce the implicit and shared assumption in hookup culture that all "romantic" relationships are long-term and monogamous. Their mononormative conflation of "romantic" with monogamy is revealed later when they write, "FWBRs might represent an intermediate position between exclusively dating and totally terminated. Again, this suggests that some FWBRs represent an intermediate position between friendships and romantic interactions" (Mongeau *et al.* 2013: 40). This interpretation of the data reflects and maintains the mononormative assumption that non-monogamous, on-going sexual relationships that include mutual caring are a transition toward or away from "real" or exclusive relationships rather than a legitimate relationship form in their own right.

From a *poly* epistemic position, FWBRs could be seen or discussed as a contextually specific form of *open* or consensually non-monogamous relationships, but neither Mongeau *et al.* (2013) nor their respondents have the language to identify these relationships as such. Instead, the waters are muddied and "relationship" continues to be conflated with monogamy, and FWBRs, the sort of relationship many college students want (more on this later), is perceived as not a "real" relationship but a transition. Unfortunately, the questionnaire Mongeau *et al.* (2013) administered, and their report, reinforces the ambiguity expressed by their respondents rather than clarify FWBRs as not only an interim or transitional state between "real" relationships and hooking up, but, instead, consensually non-monogamous and caring relationships.

Many studies on hooking up and campus hookup cultures rely on the Online College Social Life Survey (OCSLS). A poly gaze reveals that the questions on that survey are mononormative in that they conflate relationship with sexual exclusivity, for instance, the question: "Since you started college, with how many people have you been on dates with whom you were NOT already in a relationship?" This is followed up with the following question: "Now some questions about the last date that you went on with someone you were not already in an exclusive relationship with." The survey moves seamlessly from asking about being in a relationship to being in an "exclusive relationship." This is further reinforced with: "The following questions are about any sexual activity that occurred during your most recent date with someone you weren't already in an exclusive relationship with (the same date you've been answering questions about)."

About hookups, the survey asks, "how many people have you hooked up with in the case where you were not already in a romantic relationship with the person but you did know him or her?" Here relationship is conflated with "romantic" and, given the previous references to sexual exclusivity, this sequence of questions implicitly conflates "romantic" with sexual exclusivity. Moreover, questions about "Relationships" are in a completely separate section, and like the questions on hookups, conflate sexual exclusivity and relationships. For instance: "Since you started college have you been in a romantic relationship that has lasted longer than six months?" There is no definition of "romantic," but a subsequent question asks: "How many times did you and your significant other go out on a date before you became an exclusive couple?" Again, this sends the implicit message that all couple relationships are on the path toward and defined by sexual exclusivity.

Finally, there is a question about how the respondent knew they were in a relationship:

"How did it become clear that this person was your boyfriend or girlfriend?" The available responses include: "I initiated a talk in which we decided that it was an exclusive relationship; S/he initiated a talk in which we decided that it was an exclusive relationship; I heard him/her referring to me as 'boyfriend' or 'girlfriend'; I just sort of knew; Other." The question conveys quite clearly that a talk about sexual exclusivity is a threshold across which all relationships will eventually move in order to become "romantic," "committed," or "serious". While there are questions about respondents' attitudes about sexual exclusivity, there are no questions about whether or not participants' relationships are, in fact, sexually exclusive. Instead, it is both assumed and conveyed in the sequence and content of questions. Moreover, there are no questions on the OCSLS that include the phrase "consensually non-monogamous."

Like the OCSLS, many research instruments used in other studies follow similar patterns by using the words "romantic" or "committed" to operationalize "relationships" as distinct from "hookups." For example, Fielder, Carey, and Carey (2012) define hookups in their survey instrument as "someone whom you were not dating or in a romantic relationship with at the time of the physical intimacy and there was no mutual expectation of a romantic commitment" (657–8). While it might be the case that participants understand what Fielder and colleagues mean by "romantic" and "committed," to the extent that the participants hold a mononormative definition of "real" relationships (that they are romantic, committed, and monogamous), the wording on the survey reinforces the idea that, unless sexually exclusive, partners will not feel affectionate, romantic, or responsible for their sexual partners. To juxtapose romantic, committed, and monogamous with hooking up leaves no room for participants or the researchers to imagine, let alone analyze CNMRs. In a more recent article, James-Kangal *et al.* (2018) write,

> Participants selected their expected relationship status at two future time points using the following options: (a) single, (b) in a non-exclusive relationship, or c) in a monogamous, committed relationship (including but not limited to marriage). The first two options were combined to form the category "single/not in a committed relationship," while the latter was categorized as a "committed (or exclusive) relationship."
>
> *(714)*

The question, as written, assumes *and conveys* to participants that only sexually exclusive relationships are "committed" excluding the possibility of a committed relationship being consensually non-monogamous.

In contrast, some researchers successfully avoid mononormativity by defining hookups, not by the presence or absence of romance, affection, or commitment, but instead by level of acquaintance. For instance, Bersamin *et al.* (2014) operationalize casual sex by asking participants "how often during the past 30 days they had sex with someone they knew for less than a week" (46). Eshbaugh and Gute (2008) asked participants whether or not they had "intercourse with someone known for less than 24 hours" (82). In these instruments, there is not an implied binary between romantic and committed relationships and hookups. Instead, hookups are defined by how well the hookup partners know each other.

In studies of the gender gap in orgasms, researchers also consistently conflate monogamy with "relationships" and then conclude that women's orgasms are more likely in monogamous relationships. For example, Armstrong, England and Fogarty (2012) write in their introduction, "hooking up involves sexual activity… outside of an *exclusive relationship*" (435, emphasis added). Again, like in the studies discussed above, Armstrong, England, and Fogarty (2012) invoke monogamy as the distinguishing feature of relationships. Later, in a section entitled "Commitment and Affection," they write,

> *Commitment* may be important because it brings trust in *sexual exclusivity*, a feeling of security in the future of the relationship, or because it often accompanies affection. Mutual affection may enhance sex whether or not it is accompanied by a long-term commitment.
>
> *(437, emphasis added)*

Here, they move seamlessly from discussing "exclusive" relationships to "committed" relationships, leaving out the possibility that relationships can be affectionate, endure over time, and be open or consensually non-monogamous. Moreover, by conflating "commitment," "sexual exclusivity," and sexual pleasure for women, they reinforce the mononormative assumption in hookup culture that interpersonal responsibility and accountability *require* monogamy. Although it is not unreasonable to assume that sexual exclusivity would lead to trust and "feelings of security," Armstrong *et al.* articulate the mononormative assumption that affection and commitment are synonymous with monogamy. This is somewhat puzzling given their data show "women...most frequently had orgasms when they were with a caring sexual partner, he was concerned with her pleasure, willing to take time and perform the practices that worked, and she could communicate about what felt good" (Armstrong, England, and Fogarty 2012: 454). They go on to state, "Women we interviewed did not attribute their greater enjoyment of relationship sex to commitment or a future, but rather to affection and caring" (455). Finally, given the data, they conclude, "Although there was virtually no mention of the importance of commitment, women talked extensively about the role of 'caring' and 'love' in good sex" (458). In other words, college women in their sample did not say a long-term, monogamous relationship is necessary for good sex; they said affection and kindness were, but they can't seem to get either by hooking up.

These findings are significant in that they show monogamy is neither sufficient nor necessary for women's sexual pleasure, and yet Armstrong, England, and Fogarty (2012) include "sexual exclusivity" as a defining difference between relationships and hooking up.

From a poly perspective—one in which "relationship" and all the responsibilities assumed therein are not equated with sexual exclusivity on the one hand and non-monogamy is not assumed to be "no strings attached" on the other—the problem is not the lack of sexual exclusivity, but instead, the *prohibition* on caring, having some mutual responsibility, and feeling affection for each other in the context of non-monogamy.

When researchers implicitly send the message to their study participants and readers, which often include college students, that "relationship" is synonymous with monogamy, they reinforce the idea that mutual respect, gender egalitarianism, women's sexual pleasure, and men's accountability should be expected and experienced only within the context of monogamous relationships. This encourages women who want to be treated well by their sexual partners to pursue monogamous relationships with individual men. It also perpetuates the idea that, unless sexual relations take place in a sexually exclusive relationship, men do not have to engage in emotional labor or take some responsibility for their partners' sexual pleasure.

This message, conveyed in the research literature, is significant because much of the research on campus sexual cultures shows quite clearly that most participants endorse hooking up precisely because it is *not monogamous* and allows sexual exploration outside of the context long-term, monogamous relationships. For instance, Aubrey and Smith (2013) find that, despite men's advantage and women's disadvantage, the majority of college students endorse hooking up as a legitimate practice and do so because of its associations with American values of autonomy, having fun, and control over one's sexuality. Many college students embrace the non-monogamy of hookup culture to delay adulthood (Bogle 2008; Lamont 2014) because they do not want to take on adult responsibilities and, instead, they want to have "fun" and "party" and hooking up is, for many, very much associated with both (Aubrey and Smith 2013; Wade 2017). Moreover, college students place a great deal of value on socializing in groups and cultivating inter-gender relationships, and they perceive monogamous coupling as contradictory to or closing off socializing with and forming close ties with friends.

At the same time, both men and women find that some aspects of hooking up are dissatisfying. For example, contrary to the gender assumptions made by participants about what women and men want, research suggests that men desire, seek, and enjoy close emotional ties with their sexual partners as much as women do (Bay-Cheng, Robinson, and Zucker 2009; Epstein *et al.* 2009; Manning, Longore, and Giordono 2006). Interestingly, research on "friends with benefits relationships" (FWBRs) suggests that sex within the context of on-going, *non-monogamous*, heterosexual relationships can serve men's and women's needs and desires and minimize the gender inequalities of "one and done" hookups. FWBRs, in other words, appear to come closest to what many college students are seeking—affection, trust, sexual pleasure, and no expectation for sexual exclusivity (Bisson and Levine 2009; Epstein *et al.* 2009; Hughes, Morrison, and Asada 2005; Mongeau *et al.* 2013). In their study of FWBRs, Bay-Cheng *et al.* (2009) conclude:

> Our findings offer quantitative support for speculation that FWBRs may enable individuals to enjoy the stability, familiarity and egalitarian balance of platonic friendships as a means of sexual experimentation and gratification without the difficulties (e.g. volatility, power differences) and constraints (e.g. monogamy) associated with romantic relationships…Although these data lead us to dispute the popular assumption that romance is a necessary component of a healthy, functional, and positive sexual experience, they also seem to suggest that some sort of intimacy is.
>
> *(520–521)*

Research on FWBRs shows that many college students want some interpersonal connection with their sexual partners, but, at the same time, they do not want to compromise their ability to "see what's out there," by "settling" into monogamous, dyadic relationships that close off their ability to cultivate inter and intra-gender friendships (Aubrey and Smith 2013; Epstein *et al.* 2009). FWBRs are, for all intents and purposes, a relationship form that differs from one-and-done hookups *and* long-term, monogamous relationships. In other words, many college students are already engaging in consensually non-monogamous relationships and find them to be an optimal strategy for getting their sexual, interpersonal, and social needs met. However, research on FWBRs also clearly shows that most college students do not have a language for ethical and consensual non-monogamy that explicitly includes interpersonal responsibility and accountability and open communication.

> About half of the participants indicated that questions arose in their FWB relationship, and these questions involved uncertainty about what to call the relationship, the future of the relationship, and how to negotiate changes in feelings. Despite these uncertainties, however, participants reported little talk about the state of the relationship. Almost 85% indicated that no relationship talk was initiated and 73% indicated no discussion of relationship ground rules. Of the relatively few participants who explicitly established ground rules, the most prevalent theme involved third party concerns related to disclosing the relationship to others and establishing that they, unlike exclusively dating couples, were allowed to see other people. Specific strategies involved seeking compromise and arguing for one's own desired outcome. No significant sex differences in communication patterns were found, possibly due to the low frequency talk about the state and future of the relationship. While previous research has also reported that taboo topics are prevalent in relationships, the current findings suggest that this is especially true for FWB relationships.
>
> *(Bisson and Levine 2009: 71)*

As Bisson and Levine's research suggests, not only is there little discussion of the parameters of relationships among friends with benefits (FWB); the most common topic of conversation between FWB is whether or not to disclose the relationship for fear that others will assume they are monogamous thereby closing off opportunities to hookup with others. Aware of the mononormative assumptions made by their peers, FWB often keep their relationships secret further perpetuating the idea that all relationships are monogamous. In sum, FWBRs are a relatively common non-monogamous relationship strategy adopted by American college students, but they often remain hidden and campus sexual cultures do not include a language for *ethical* on-going, affectionate, and non-monogamous relationships.

Research with a poly gaze and the possibilities of poly hookup cultures?

It is not inevitable that research reports on hookup culture reproduce the mononormative assumption that monogamy is necessary for good, healthy relationships and that non-monogamy leads to gender inequality. For instance, two books, *American Hookup* by Lisa Wade (2017) and Donna Freitas's (2013) *The End of Sex* are examples of how researchers can successfully analyze relationships, hookup culture, and gender and avoid mononormativity in their interpretation and description of their data and findings. Donna Freitas (2013), for example, writes,

An effective response to hookup culture could be as simple as inviting students to apply critical-thinking skills to the task of evaluating their weekend activities; asking them to draw on their on-campus experiences as they discuss gender, politics, philosophy, literature, theology, education, and social justice inside the classroom.

(185)

Rather than presenting monogamous coupling as an antidote to gender inequality in hookup culture, Freitas encourages critical thinking about those dynamics. One critical perspective could be developed by, for instance, encouraging college students to adopt a poly gaze, not to necessarily form polyamorous relationships (although that would be an option), but to gain perspective on the workings of mononormativity and compulsory monogamy in the gender dynamics in heterosexual campus hookup cultures.

Introducing a poly gaze to campus sexual cultures could challenge the idea that casual sex *cannot* include caring feelings, mutual responsibility, and open communication, and more important, that these features of relationships cannot be expected or demanded in the context of non-monogamy. Lisa Wade (2017) writes:

> Casual sex…doesn't have to be cold. If partners are invested in mutual consent and pleasure and are gracious and friendly afterward, one could say they have been nice to each other. But somewhere students lost sight of this possibility. Instead, non-exclusive relationships are assumed to lack not only love, but all the kindnesses that come with it, both small and large.
>
> *(145)*

Here, Wade states explicitly that the problem is not non-monogamy; the problem is equating monogamy with kindness and non-monogamy with being cold and unfeeling. She goes on to say:

> Students wish they had more options. Some pine for the going-steady lifestyle of the 1950's. Many mourn the antiracist, feminist utopia that their grandparents envisioned but never saw fully realized. Quite a few would like things to be a lot more queer. Some want a hookup culture that is warmer: where students aren't just poly—hooking up with multiple partners—but poly*amorous*—hooking up with multiple partners who are loving toward them.
>
> *(Wade 2017: 246, italics in original)*

According to Wade (2017), this is a problem with the cultural norms and beliefs around relationships and sex. She writes, "Seeing what's happening on campus as a culture—recognizing that it's not the hookup itself, but hookup culture that is the problem—is the first step to changing it. Because culture is a type of shared consciousness, change has to happen collectively" (247).

Much about hookup culture must change, but from a poly perspective offering something other than mononormative definitions of relationships could be one positive change. The collective understandings, norms, and ethics for doing consensual, non-monogamous relationships, especially those found in polyamory, can provide a framework for introducing a language for ethical non-monogamy in campus sexual cultures. As a relationship and sexual subculture, polyamorists have developed their own language and set of shared meanings and norms for how to do consensual, non-monogamous relationships that include affection, romance, and mutual interpersonal responsibility (Barker and Ritchie 2006). On-line forums (e.g. Polyamory Forum.com[2]), blogs (e.g. More Than Two[3]), and podcasts (e.g. Polyamory Weekly), as well as a number of "how-to" books (e.g. Anapol 2004; Anapol 2010; Block 2008; Easton and Hardy 2009; Taormino 2008; Veaux and Rickert 2014) outline the subcultural norms and ethics of polyamory. These books, podcasts, blogs, and on-line forums consistently and without exception outline ethical polyamory as including, 1) gender egalitarianism, 2) open communication to define and negotiate relationships, and 3) personal and interpersonal responsibility and accountability within the context of non-monogamy. For example, in their book, *More Than Two: A Practical Guide to Ethical Polyamory*, Franklin Veaux and Eve Rickert summarize the characteristics of contemporary poly ethics.

> Multiple romantic relationships are as old as the human race, but modern polyamory is new in a lot of ways. It's rooted in the modern values of gender equality and self-determination. It places high value on introspection, transparent communication and compassionate treatment of others.
>
> *(Veaux and Rickert 2014: 397)*

Elisabeth Sheff (2014) writes,

> One of the most distinguishing characteristics of polyamory is that it allows women multiple partners...Being able to set firm boundaries and make relationship requirements is both a source and expression of power that is denied women in most traditional or patriarchal marriages.
>
> *(28)*

In most of the available materials on consensual non-monogamy and polyamory, there is an explicitly stated expectation that men and women have equal access to other partners and that the double standard that limits women's sexual agency and autonomy is out-dated and unacceptable. In their book, *The Ethical Slut: A Practical Guide to Polyamory, Open Relationships and Other Adventures*, Dossie Easton and Janet Hardy encourage women to reject conventional ideas about femininity and desire.

> Most women are not very good at saying "yes," and not very good at saying "no"—your authors aren't, and we've been practicing both for a long time.

We're not sure how things got to this state, where a woman is just supposed to stand there looking adorable until some big strong hunk comes and makes her decision for her, but we don't like it much…Many women…can benefit greatly from learning to be more assertive in asking for what they want, both during the meeting process and afterward.

(Easton and Hardy 2009: 88)

To the extent that gender egalitarianism and a rejection of the double standard is central to poly ethics (though, perhaps, not always practiced by individuals), it offers an alternative to the existing gender dynamics in hookup culture.

Furthermore, poly ethics emphasize open and straightforward communication about relationship boundaries and expectations. In her book, *Opening Up: A Guide to Creating and Sustaining Open Relationships*, Tristan Taormino (2008) writes, "Obviously, communication is a critical part of any kind of relationship, but when it comes to nonmonogamous relationships, good communication is one of the most important skills you can have" (36). Veaux and Rickert (2014) agree:

No two people have the same needs. Whenever we tie our lives to others, especially in romantic relationships, there will be times when we can't have everything we want. The ability to negotiate in good faith and to seek compromise when our needs and those of others conflict is a vital relationship skill…The best compromises are those that allow everyone to have their needs met in ethical, compassionate ways.

(153–154)

Easton and Hardy (2009) write, "[People in non-monogamous relationships] are *honest*—with ourselves and others…We are *respectful* of others' feelings, and when we aren't sure how someone feels, we ask" (21, emphasis in original). Unlike in campus hookup cultures where most people assume that defining parameters and open communication are only required within the context of monogamous, long-term relationships, polyamorists suggest that open communication and defining parameters are *especially necessary* within the context of non-monogamy.

Finally, when it comes to treating partners ethically, poly subculture does not distinguish "casual" relationships from "serious" ones. For instance, Easton and Hardy (2009) straightforwardly endorse FWBRs, not as a transitional phase, but as a legitimate relationship strategy requiring mutually ethical treatment of partners.

The cultural ban on having sex with your friends is an inevitable offshoot of a societal belief that the only acceptable reason to have sex is to lead to a monogamous marriagelike [sic] relationship. We believe, on the other hand, that friendship is an excellent reason to have sex and that sex is an excellent way to maintain a friendship…With practice, we can develop an intimacy based on warmth and mutual respect, much freer than desperation, neediness, or the blind insanity of falling in love—that's why the relationships between "friends with benefits" are so immensely valuable. When we acknowledge that love and respect and appreciation that we share with lovers we would never marry, sexual friendships can become not only possible, but preferred.

(48)

Breaking down the distinction between "casual" hookup and "serious" relationship, Easton and Hardy (2009) explicitly state that all sexual interactions require respect and caring behavior.

Our monogamy-centrist culture tends to assume that the purpose and ultimate goal of all relationships—and all sex—is a lifelong pair bonding…We on the other hand, think sexual pleasure can certainly contribute to love, commitment, and long-term stability, if that's what you want. But those are hardly the only good reasons for having sex…A sexual relationship may last for an hour or two. It's still a relationship; the participants have related to one another—as sex partners, companions, lovers—for the duration of their interaction.

(24)

Polyamory and open relationships collapse the binary between non-monogamy and "relationship" and offer an alternative form of non-monogamy that includes both caring and interpersonal responsibility.

These features of polyamory ethics—a rejection of the double standard, gender egalitarianism, direct communication, and an expectation of mutually caring and respectful treatment of partners regardless of the presence of sexual exclusivity and/or a long term commitment—provide a starting point for thinking through what a contextually specific and life-stage appropriate *ethical* hookup culture might look like.

A more poly hookup culture would mean that the perks of relationships would not exclude hooking up and the benefits of hooking up would not preclude having meaningful and sexually satisfying but temporary relationships. Moreover, women's desire for caring and respectful treatment, as well as open communication, would no longer be conflated with a desire to "tie down" men in monogamous relationships, and individual men might be less likely to treat women badly to signal a lack of interest in an on-going monogamous relationship because 1) there would not be the mononormative expectation that "relationship" is synonymous with sexual exclusivity, and 2) women would be more likely to interpret disrespectful and selfish treatment by men, not as a desire for sex, but instead, as a power strategy and/or an effort to avoid emotional labor.

Finally, one of the biggest problems with hookup culture and friends with benefits is the lack of communication about the nature of relationships and what having sex means. Because poly ethics emphasize communication, in a more poly hookup culture conversations about the nature of relationships and intentions would be expected in all contexts, not just in a transitional phase to a long term, monogamous relationship. This kind of communication could undermine men's power advantage by eliminating the need for women to "read into" what seeing a partner with someone else means. Rather a poly approach to hooking up would encourage women to explicitly state what they want and demand that men do the same. If nothing else, introducing a model for how to do ethical non-monogamy to campus sexual cultures would lay bare men's interest in avoiding emotional labor and women's desire for caring and fair treatment. It would provide a language with which college students who participate in hookup culture and researchers who study them could challenge the idea that women want monogamy and men want sex.

Conclusion

Heterosexual hookup culture is a pervasive aspect of contemporary, American campus sexual cultures. Many college students regardless of gender seem to want to focus on their studies, have fun in a party atmosphere, socialize in large groups, and experiment with sex rather than form monogamous, marriage-like relationships (Hamilton and Armstrong 2009). Contrary to gender stereotypes circulating among college students, women and men want to have autonomy and freedom to "see what's out there," but they also want to cultivate interpersonal and emotional connections with each other. While hooking up in current campus sexual cultures provides the former, it is not conducive to the latter. Instead, hookup culture includes a set of norms that inhibit the formation of egalitarian, affectionate, and mutually beneficial relationships among hookup partners. As has been documented in the growing research literature on campus hookup cultures, this systematically works to the advantage of high-status straight men and to the disadvantage of everyone else.

From a poly perspective, however, these features of hookup culture result from the assumption that interpersonal accountability and responsibility are only required and expected within the context of sexually exclusive relationships. The mononormative conflation of non-monogamy with "no strings attached" is the foundation upon which norms against communication between hookup partners are built. The idea that sexual exclusivity is necessary for ethical treatment between sexual partners leads young women to expect and tolerate maltreatment by their hookup partners, excuses men from treating their partners well, and masks how disrespectful treatment is deployed as a strategy to maintain power and control.

It is not surprising that, for college students and many researchers, the definition of "real," "serious," or "romantic" relationships hinges on the presence or absence of sexual exclusivity. These definitions and assumptions are not limited to college campuses, but are pervasive and normative in U.S. culture more broadly and in which campuses are located. Compulsory monogamy is embedded within and constitutive of hegemonic gender relations more generally but, because of mononormativity, it remains invisible and thus unexamined by most college students and many researchers (Schippers 2016). It is for this reason that I have presented the poly gaze as a potentially valuable resource for college students and an epistemic perspective for researchers precisely because it offers a vision for gender equality, open communication, and mutual affection within the context of non-monogamous relationships.

Certainly, it is likely if not inevitable that those who benefit from gender inequality, limited communication, and maltreatment of sexual partners, most notably high-status and privileged heterosexual men will resist changes in campus sexual cultures. However, despite the inevitable resistance of some, access to a poly gaze would at least provide a language for ethical non-monogamy and shine a critical light on some of the obscured workings of compulsory monogamy and mononormativity in the gender dynamics and outcomes of hooking up.

Notes

1 While it must be said that most of this research focuses almost exclusively on heterosexual hookup culture, recent research is emerging and provides data on how queer young adults experience hookup culture. Significantly, this research shows that there is far more value and importance placed on consent and sexual pleasure when queer college students hookup. However, queer hookup cultures maintain the cultural prohibition on "catching feelings" through hookups seen in heterosexual hookup culture. See Lamont, Roach, and Kahn (2018).

2 www.polyamory.com/forum/.

3 http://polyweekly.com.

References

Anapol, Deborah. 2004. "A Glimpse of Harmony." *Journal of Bisexuality* 4(3–4): 109–119.

Anapol, Deborah. 2010. *Polyamory in the 21st Century: Love and Intimacy with Multiple Partners.* New York: Rowman and Littlefield.

Armstrong, Elizabeth A., Paula England, and Alison Fogarty. 2012. "Accounting for Women's Orgasm and Sexual Enjoyment in College Hookups and Relationships." *American Sociological Review* 77: 435–462.

Armstrong, Elizabeth A., Laura Hamilton, and Paula England. 2010. "Is Hooking up Bad for Young Women? Compared to What?" *Contexts* 9: 22–27.

Aubrey, Jennifer S. and Siobhan E. Smith. 2013. "Development and Validation of the Endorsement of the Hookup Culture Index." *The Journal of Sex Research* 50(5): 435–448.

Backstrom, L., Elizabeth Armstrong, and Jennifer Puentes. 2012. "Women's Negotiation of Cunnilingus in College Hookups and Relationships." *Journal of Sex Research* 49: 1–12.

Barker, Meg and Ritchie, Ani. 2006. "'There Aren't Words for What We Do or How We Feel So We Have to Make Them Up': Constructing Polyamorous Languages in a Culture of Compulsory Monogamy." *Sexualities* 9(5): 584–601.

Bay-Cheng, Laina Y., Adjoa D. Robinson, and Alyssa N. Zucker. 2009. "Behavioral and Relational Contexts of Adolescent Desire: Wanting and Pleasure; Undergraduate Women's Retrospective Accounts." *The Journal of Sex Research* 46(6): 511–524.

Bersamin, Melina, Byron Zamboanga, Seth Schwartz, M. Brent Donnellan, Monika Hudson, Robert Weisskirch, Su Yeong Kim, V. Bede Agocha, Susan Krauss Whitbourn, and Jean Caraway. 2014. "Risky Business: Is There an Association between Casual Sex and Mental Health among Emerging Adults?" *The Journal of Sex Research* 51(1): 43–51.

Bisson, Melissa A. and Timothy R. Levine. 2009. "Negotiating a Friends with Benefits Relationship." *Archive of Sexual Behavior* 38: 66–73.

Block, Jenny. 2008. *Open: Love, Sex and Life in an Open Marriage.* Berkeley, CA: Seal Press.

Bogle, Kathleen A. 2008. *Hooking Up: Sex, Dating, and Relationships on Campus.* New York: New York University Press.

Bradshaw, Carolyn, Arnold S. Kahn, and Bryan K. Saville, 2010. "To Hook Up or Date: Which Gender Benefits?" *Sex Roles*, 62(9–10): 661–669.

Easton, Dossie and Janet W. Hardy. 2009. *The Ethical Slut: A Practical Guide to Polyamory, Open Relationships, and Other Adventures*, 2nd edn. Berkeley, CA: Celestial Arts.

England, Paula, Emily Fitzgibbons Shafer, and Alison C. K. Fogarty. 2007. "Hooking Up and Forming Romantic Relationships on Today's College Campuses." In M. Kimmel (Ed), *The Gendered Society Reader.* New York: Oxford University Press.

England, Paula and Reuben J. Thomas. 2006. "The Decline of the Date and the Rise of the College Hook Up." In Arlene S. Skolnick and Jerome H. Skolnick (Eds), *The Family in Transition.* Boston, MA: Allyn & Bacon.

Epstein, Marina, Jerel P. Calzo, Andrew P. Smiler, and L. Monique Ward. 2009. "Anything from Making Out to Having Sex: Men's Negotiations of Hooking Up and Friends-with-benefits Scripts." *Journal of Sex Research* 46: 414–424.

Eshbaugh, Elaine M. and Gary Gute. 2008. "Hookups and Sexual Regret among College Women." *Journal of Social Psychology* 148: 77–89.

Fielder, Robyn L. and Michael P. Carey. 2010. "Predictors and Consequences of Sexual "Hookups" among College Students: A Short-Term Prospective Study." *Archives of Sexual Behavior* 39(5): 1105–1119.

Fielder, Robyn L., Kate B. Carey, and Michael P. Carey. 2012. "Are Hookups Replacing Romantic Relationships? A Longitudinal Study of First-year Female College Students." *Journal of Adolescent Health* 52(5): 657–659.

Freitas, Donna. 2013. *The End of Sex: How Hookup Culture Is Leaving a Generation Unhappy, Sexually Unfulfilled, and Confused About Intimacy.* New York: Basic Books.

Gilmartin, Shannon K. 2007. "Crafting Heterosexual Masculine Identities on Campus: College Men Talk About Romantic Love." *Men and Masculinities* 9: 530–539.

Hamilton, Laura and Elizabeth A. Armstrong. 2009. "Gendered Sexuality in Young Adulthood: Double Binds and Flawed Options." *Gender & Society* 23: 589–616.

Heldman, Caroline and Lisa Wade. 2010. "Hook-up Culture: Setting a New Research Agenda." *Sexuality Research and Social Policy* 7: 323–333.

Hughes, Mikayla, Kelly Morrison, and Kelli Jean K. Asada. 2007. "What's Love Got to Do with It? Exploring the Impact of Maintenance Rules, Love Attitudes, and Network Support on Friends with Benefits Relationships." *Western Journal of Communication* 69(1): 49–66.

James-Kangal, Neslihan, Eliza Weitbrecht, Trenel Francis, and Sarah Whitton. 2018. "Hooking Up and Emerging Adults' Relationship Attitudes and Expectations." *Sexuality & Culture* 22(3): 706–723.

Kelly, Conor. 2012. "Sexism in Practice: Feminist Ethics Evaluating the Hookup Culture." *Journal of Feminist Studies in Religion* 28(2): 27–48.

Kimmel, Michael. 2008. *Guyland: The Perilous World Where Boys Become Men: Understanding the Critical Years between 16 and 26.* New York: HarperCollins.

Kreager, Derek and Jeremy Staff. 2009. "The Sexual Double Standard and Adolescent Peer Acceptance." *Social Psychology Quarterly* 72: 143–164.

Lamont, Ellen. 2014. "Negotiating Courtship: Reconciling Egalitarian Ideals with Traditional Gender Norms." *Gender & Society* 28(2): 189–211.

Lamont, Ellen, Teresa Roach, and Sope Kahn. 2018. "Navigating Campus Hookup Culture: LGBTQ Students and College Hookups." *Sociological Forum* 33(4): 1000–1022.

Manning, Wendy D., Monica A. Longmore, and Peggy C. Giordano. 2005. "Adolescents' Involvement in Non-Romantic Sexual Activity." *Social Science Research* 34: 384–407.

Manning, Wendy D., Peggy C. Giordano, and Monica A. Longmore. 2006. "Hooking Up: The Relationship Contexts of Nonrelationship Sex." *Journal of Adolescent Research* 21: 459–483.

Mint, Pepper. 2004. "The Power Dynamics of Cheating." *Journal of Bisexuality* 4(3–4): 55–76.

Mongeau, Paul A., Kendra Knight, Jade Williams, Jennifer Eden, and Christina Shaw. 2013. "Identifying and Explicating Variation among Friends With Benefits Relationships." *The Journal of Sex Research* 50(1): 37–47.

Pieper, Marianne and Robin Bauer. 2005. Call for papers: International Conference on Polyamory and Mono-normativity. Research Centre for Feminist, Gender & Queer Studies, University of Hamburg, November 5–6, 2005.

Reid, Julie A., Sinikka Elliott, and Gretchen R. Webber. 2011. "Casual Hookups to Formal Dates: Refining the Boundaries of The Sexual Double Standard." *Gender & Society* 25: 545–568.

Regnerus, Mark and Jeremy Uecker. 2011. *Premarital Sex in America: How Young Americans Meet, Mate, and Think about Marrying*. New York: Oxford University Press.

Sales, Nancy Jo. 2018. *Swiped: Hooking Up in the Digital Age*. Documentary Film: HBO.

Schippers, Mimi. 2016. *Beyond Monogamy: Polyamory and The Future of Polyqueer Sexualities*. New York: New York University Press.

Sheff, Elisabeth. 2014. *The Polyamorist Next Door: Inside Multiple-Partner Relationships and Families*. New York: Rowman and Littlefield.

Taormino, Tristan. 2008. *Opening up: A Guide to Creating and Sustaining Open Relationships*. San Francisco, CA: Cleis Press.

Wade, Lisa. 2017. *American Hookup: The New Culture of Sex on Campus*. New York: W.W. Norton & Company.

Wade, Lisa and Caroline Heldman. 2012. "Hooking Up and Opting Out: Negotiating Sex in the First Year of College." In Carpenter, Laura and John DeLamater (Eds), *Sex for Life: From Virginity to Viagra, How Sexuality Changes throughout Our Lives*. New York: New York University Press.

Veaux, Franklin and Eve Rickert. 2014. *More than Two: A Practical Guide to Polyamory*. Portland, OR: Thorntree Press.

4

HISTORICAL BIOGRAPHY AND THE ERASURE OF POLY PASTS

Introduction

One morning, I was listening to National Public Radio's *Fresh Air with Terry Gross*. Her guest was historian Jill Lepore, and they were discussing her book, *The Secret History of Wonder Woman* (Lepore 2014). I have never been a fan of comic books, including *Wonder Woman*, but I was interested in the feminist content of the original comic and how it reflected the creator's life and politics. In 1941, when All Star Comics introduced Wonder Woman, William Moulton Marston was committed to "equality of the sexes," thought women were superior to men, and desired a world run by women and ruled by "female" values such as peace, community, and nurturing rather than war, competition, and selfishness. The National Public Radio interview up to that point was interesting—Lepore is a brilliant scholar and engaging interviewee, and Terry Gross was her usual, insightful interlocutor. Then Terry Gross asked Lepore about Marston's home life.

Marston, Lepore explained, had two wives, Elizabeth Holloway and Olive Byrne. They all lived in the same home with their children and, according to Lepore's sources, each of the adults had their own bedrooms connected by a shared bathroom through which Marston could access the beds of both women, which he did (Lepore 2014: 154). Of course this meant that the women could access each other's bedrooms as well, but the focus of the interview was William Marston.

I immediately stopped what I was doing and turned up the volume on my radio. Holloway, Byrne, and Marston were in a marriage-like relationship, shared a home, and raised their children together. In my mind, this meant only one thing. *Marston was poly!*

As is always the case when I learn of figures from the past and present who were or are poly (and by "poly" I mean having intimate relationships with more than one other person, not necessarily polyamorous in contemporary terms), I feel a sense of connection—dare I say queer kinship. *My people!* And here were Terry Gross and Jill Lepore talking about it on the usually conventional National Public Radio. For a moment, I heard them saying to me, "Hey you, poly person, we're talking about the feminist creator of Wonder Woman, and he was poly, just like you!" I felt, in a word, hailed.

But then, as it so often does, the other shoe dropped. In need of some explanation for this, in Gross's words, "bizarre" arrangement, Lepore said, "[Marston] at that point has developed some pretty unconventional ideas about sex and gender that come from his work as a psychologist and from other kinds of proclivities that I think are unreachable to the historian" (NPR 2017). To this, Gross laughed out loud. Later, Lepore described the family arrangement as "this crazy bohemian thing." Through befuddled snickering, Gross agreed that the Marstons were "this unconventional family with this huge secret." I recognized in myself the sinking disappointment in realizing they were gawking at, not hailing, me.

The disappointment was compounded when Gross suggested that Marston's feminism was a contradiction to his family life. She said in the interview:

> Because William Marston really believed in women's rights, and the suffrage movement was kind of formative for him—you know, he put a lot of that into *Wonder Woman*. But, you know, at home, he has basically two wives, a wife and a mistress. He has children with both of them. And I keep asking myself, was he being very sexist and—you know, at home by having, like, two wives, basically? Or was this a good arrangement for the two women?
>
> *(NPR 2017)*

I bristled when Gross referred to Olive Byrne as the "mistress" and Elizabeth Holloway as "the wife."

Without saying so explicitly, Lepore challenged Gross's interpretation in this rather long explanation of how the Marston's family life could be consistent with feminism.

> I have two things to say. One is that when Holloway does write these letters in 1963 saying what it was like…She says, look. You know, we both loved him. And he loved us. And there was love-making for all. That's the phrase she uses. And the kids all say it was actually a delightful way to grow up—that they were deeply loved by everybody in different ways. So I actually think that it'd be better…to…look at the larger culture and say, look. Why do people still joke—I'm sure you have friends—heterosexual couples—who are both working and raising kids who say, sheesh, you know what we need? We need a wife [laughter], you know, to stay home and take care of the kids. But that is actually—still remains a problem—that the basic, structural problems that are attendant on thinking about women as political actors and women as economic actors on a stage of equality with men have never yet been solved.

And they have actually been barely addressed. In fact, they're put to one side by each generation. And there are all these crazy patches that are patched all on top of these problems. And so I love the family story. I think it's fascinating [laughter]. It's dramatic and interesting. But I hope that what it causes people to reflect on is the duration and the stubbornness and the lack of advance in this struggle for women's equality.

(NPR 2017)

Lepore, it appears, sees the family arrangement as loving, good for the kids, and a sort of remedy for the problem of the second shift in which employed women have to do a double shift of childcare and housework when they come home from their jobs. Then Lepore described how Holloway and Byrne lived together for 30 years after William Marston died. The rest of the family referred to them as "the ladies," and they were "inseparable…went everywhere together [and] were devoted to each other" (NPR 2017). It turns out Olive Byrne was a lot more than Marston's "mistress," and Elizabeth Holloway benefited greatly from her relationship with Byrne. Ultimately, Lepore suggests that we really can't know what was in the hearts of Holloway, Byrne, and Marston.

Historians have different procedures and methods and ways to think about what we can know and what we can't know and what our obligations are. But my general premise is these people lived and died. Their children know them better than I do. Unless I have documentary evidence that tells me one thing or another, I'm not confident to draw a conclusion.

(NPR 2017)

Lepore's biography is very much about Marston's personal life. The "secret" in the title, *The Secret History of Wonder Woman*, is, in fact, polyamory. And despite her sympathetic rendering of Olive Byrne and Elizabeth Holloway in her interview on *Fresh Air*, in the book Lepore suggests that, for William Marston, the poly arrangement contradicted his commitment to equality between the sexes.

After reading *The Secret History of Wonder Woman* with a poly gaze, I came to different conclusions. Lepore's rendering of the Marston family is mono-normative—meaning, it renders non-monogamous and polyamorous relationships as deviant, a perverted spectacle, and thus, evidence of psychological pathology. She never comes right out and says so, but a close analysis of her language, presumptions, and conclusions shows that she interprets the Marstons through a mono rather than a poly gaze. And Lepore is not alone. Many contemporary historical biographers "read" their subjects' non-monogamous or poly lives through a mono lens. When confronted with evidence of something other than monogamous coupling, historical biographers too often interpret their data in ways that render non-monogamy pathological, ridiculous, or impossible.

My goals with this chapter are twofold. First, I revisit contemporary biographies of historical figures who rejected monogamous coupling to analyze how biographers describe and interpret what, from a poly perspective, looks a lot like polyamory in the lives of these figures. What we shall see is that many historical biographers interpret non-monogamous and polyamorous figures with a mononormative gaze, not a poly one.

They often rely too heavily on psychological needs or pathology to explain the relationship choices of their historical subjects and miss the political and sociological significance of living an *anti-monogamous* life (see Willey 2016).

In my analyses of the historical biographies covered in this chapter, I do not take issue with the veracity of authors' work. In fact, having not done the archival and interview research myself, I do not have the qualifications or the data to question whether or not each of the biographers was correct on the facts. Instead, I analyze *how* the authors interpret the facts by focusing on the specific language they use, the interpretations they offer, and the conclusions they draw. I hope that, by doing so, I can offer a model of sorts for how others can adopt a poly gaze to read other historical biographies.

The second goal of this chapter is to reclaim, in a sense, poly figures from the past in order to begin building a poly archive. As I said, I feel a queer kinship with these figures, and as a polyamorous person, I want to reclaim them. This, of course, is a project that many gay, lesbian, bisexual, and trans★ people have been doing for decades. They argue that it is important to identify how heteronormative assumptions shape the way in which straight biographers interpret queerness and reclaim figures from the past as anti or non-heteronormative so as to challenge the myth that heterosexuality is natural, inevitable, and desirable across time and cultures. With an eye toward avoiding interpreting events from the past through contemporary concepts and assumptions, my goal is not to claim that I know the hearts and minds of these figures. Instead, my goal is to illustrate how contemporary biographies are mononormative and to offer an alternative reading of the historical evidence the authors provide. I'm not so much mining for polyamorous people; I am mining for contemporary examples of mononormativity in historical biographies of figures from the past that, in whatever shape, form, or fashion, lived anti-monogamous lives. I begin with an in-depth look at Lepore's book. I then move to biographies of Emma Goldman and E.E. Cummings to offer other examples of mononormative historical biography. Finally, I discuss biographies of Audre Lorde and Edna St. Vincent Millay to show that mononormativity is not inevitable.

Lepore's *The Secret History of Wonder Woman*

Lepore's (2014) biography is a beautifully written, engaging, detailed, and well-researched description of William Marston's life. Her main goal in the book is to connect Marston's biography to the creation and content of *Wonder Woman* comics, and to that effect, she is quite successful. The facts, as reported by Lepore are that William Marston married Elizabeth Holloway in September, 1915. Soon after, Lepore surmises some time in 1919, Marston met Marjorie

Wilkes Harvey at Camp Upton, New York. He was there to treat shell shock victims, and Harvey was the camp librarian. Lepore (2014) writes, "Marston was twenty-five and far from his wife; Huntley was twenty-nine and divorced. They were together for six months" (58). After returning home to Holloway, Harvey came to visit. Lepore (2014) writes, "Marston had left her with an understanding that she ought to come whenever she liked. She talked, later, about how she and Marston and Holloway became a 'threesome'" (58). Later, Holloway and Marston met Olive Byrne, invited her to be his research assistant, and eventually, Olive Byrne moved in with them. According to Lepore, it was Marston's idea, and when faced with his request, Holloway said she would go along with the arrangement as long as Byrne raised the children and Holloway could pursue her career. Indeed, Byrne raised her and Holloway's children, all fathered by Marston, and Holloway was the main economic provider to the household. Holloway named one of her children Olive Ann, and Holloway and Marston legally adopted Olive Byrne's children, giving them the name Marston.

There are three ways in which Lepore's portrait of the Marston family life is mononormataive. The first, and perhaps most important, conclusion that Lepore draws is that the Marston family arrangement was controlled by William and served his selfish and perverted interests. It is difficult to overstate the snicker in Lepore's prose whenever she describes Marston's over-indulgent interest in women and sex.

> Marston first revealed his fascination with sex and sexual difference in an article he published in the *Journal of Experimental Psychology* at the end of 1923…He'd wanted to discover in what ways women's brains work differently than men's. He and Holloway had conducted blood pressure tests on ten men and ten women. They'd tried to get them upset, and then they'd tried to arouse them…what this kind of research had most clearly proved to Marston was how much he liked doing this kind of research, especially the part about getting women excited.
>
> *(Lepore 2014: 111)*

There is no doubt that, at the time, research on sexuality and arousal was outside the norm. Rather than perceive Marston and Holloway's research as groundbreaking, Lepore dismisses it as lascivious.

Casting Marston as perverted is a running theme throughout the book. Describing a book that Marston gave Holloway as a gift, Lepore (2014) writes, "Marston liked these lines: 'I saw a cat—'twas but a dream/Who scorned the slave that brought her cream.' It sounds a little filthy. In the margin, Marston wrote, 'Ha!Ha!'" (43). The word "filthy" is not a neutral term and implicitly reinforces Lepore's take on Marston's sexuality. Lepore (2014) even goes so far as to suggest that there was something incestuous about the family.

> Marston was devoted and passionately affectionate, maybe too affectionate. Every night, he insisted that O.A. enter his study, say "Goodnight Daddy," and kiss him on the mouth. Every night, she refused. "For Christ's sake," Olive would say, "just run in there and kiss him quick and get it over with."
>
> *(176)*

The taint of poly perversion becomes the lens through which Lepore (2014) interprets all of Marston's work, *despite* his political commitment to Eros and women's empowerment.

> In 1931, he talked to a reporter about coeds. "He believes the sexes have changed their professional status," the reporter said, "that the hunted has become the huntress, that men students have more ideas about women than about themselves and that a majority of men prefer to be 'unhappy masters' rather than 'happy slaves.'" Maybe it was Marston who was, in those years, an unhappy master.
>
> *(148)*

Describing a photograph of Holloway, Byrne, Marston, and Ethel Byrne, on the day of Olive Byrne's graduation, Lepore (2014) writes, "It's a family photograph but a bewildering one: Marston and Holloway look as if they must be Olive Byrne's parents, except that they're too young. [They were only eleven years older than she was.] Ethel Byrne looks as though she might be an aunt" (116). The photo is bewildering to Lepore because she's interpreting it through a mononormative lens that can only see "family" if it looks like a two-parent, dependent children nuclear family. From a poly perspective, however, it is not at all bewildering because the photo depicts a polyamorous triad. *Seeing* poly kinship in the photo is *not* bewildering; it hails and pleases.

To the extent that Lepore explains the poly arrangement as a result of Marston's own perverse indulgences and unhealthy interest in sex, she makes a second mononormative assumption by painting the women as unwilling and exploited by the situation.

> The year Margaret Sanger won her greatest victory [The American Medical Association endorsed birth control, and Marston suggested would make matriarchy inevitable] and William Moulton Marston held a press conference about Amazonian rule, Olive Byrne was typing his books and raising his children, and Sadie Elizabeth Holloway was supporting him. A matriarchy Cherry Orchard [the name of the home Marston, Holloway, and Byrne shared with their children] was not.
>
> *(Lepore 2014: 173)*

The tone of this paragraph is that Marston was taking advantage of Byrne and Holloway.

It is clear throughout that Lepore cannot imagine that everyone's needs could very well be met in a household that includes two wives. During the *Fresh Air* interview with Terry Gross discussed above, Lepore makes the connections between the second shift and Holloway's decision to accept Byrne into the household. In the book, however, Lepore glosses the reality that Olive Byrne was not just raising Marston's kids; she was also raising Elizabeth Holloway's children. Moreover, Holloway could support Marston precisely because she was unburdened with motherhood and housework and thus able to pursue her career.

This is significant because Lepore is not just reading the situation through a mononormative lens; she is also reading it through gender stereotypes. If a man has two wives, he must be pulling the strings because no woman would willingly choose polygamy, and he must be self-serving, dominant, and abusive. Lepore (2014) writes,

> The kids read comics. Holloway earned the money…Olive took care of everyone, stealing time to write for Family Circle. And William Moulton Marston…the [lie] detector who declared feminine rule a fact, was petted and indulged. He'd fume and he'd storm and he'd holler, and the women would whisper to the children, "It's best to ignore him."
>
> *(180)*

However, as described by Lepore (2014), the family arrangement appeared to serve everyone's needs, including the women and children.

> The family arrangement, in which Marston had two wives, one to work and one to raise the children, involved the promotion of Holloway's career. Olive Byrne had the best possible modern-day psychological training necessary for the modern, scientific management of children. Her staying home with Holloway's baby allowed Holloway to lead the life of a professional woman, unencumbered by the duties of motherhood. And Holloway's income supported Olive's children, when they came. Marston had never been able to hold a job for more than a year. He needed Holloway's income.
>
> *(145)*

There is an underlying assumption in Lepore's prose that men should be economic providers, and if they are not, they are taking advantage of whoever is economically providing for the family. Moreover, to say that "Marston had two wives," is to reproduce the idea that men possess women, but not the other way around. Given what appears to be mutual affection among the three of them, we could just as easily assume that Holloway had a husband and a wife, as did Olive Byrne. All the evidence suggests that was in fact the case, and it worked. Research on polyamorous families consistently shows that having multiple adults in the household can alleviate the burdens of housework and childcare, and, as a result, children in these households do very well (Sheff 2014; Pallotta-Chiarolli 2010).

This research also shows that, like children in gay and lesbian families, stigma can be difficult to manage for both adults and children. Many poly families feel the need to keep the family arrangement secret at least in some contexts. With no apparent understanding of what it is like to be polyamorous in a mononormative world where there are no legal protections, Lepore (2014) concludes that the secrecy around the family arrangement reflected a general propensity for deceit on the part of William Marston: "The problem with the way the Marstons lived was that their neighbors would have considered it abnormal. Olive believed the truth was best kept secret: in particular, she didn't want her children to know about it, ever" (147).

Lepore is confounded by the trio's desire to keep their life a secret and conflates being closeted with being dishonest. From a poly perspective, however, there is no inconsistency between a desire to keep a poly arrangement secret and valuing honesty within relationships. And, as Lepore (2014) suggests, honesty was of the utmost importance to Marston.

> Most heartache Marston diagnosed as the product of deceit. "In a majority of cases which are brought to me as a consulting psychologist for love or marital adjustment, there are self-deceptions to be uncovered as well as attempts to deceive other people," he explained. "Beneath such love conflicts there is almost always a festering psychological core of dishonesty."
>
> *(165)*

As a historian, Lepore masterfully situates Holloway, Byrne, and Marston in their historical time by emphasizing the fight for women's suffrage and the birth control movement to explain their feminist sensibilities. However, at the same time, she fails to contextualize their poly relationship in its historical time—a time when, as described in the last chapter, polygamy was associated with Mormon fundament-alism and deeply stigmatized, not to mention illegal. Of course they were secretive about their arrangement.

Instead of seeing their poly arrangement as a historically specific remedy to the gender structure of work and family, and as consistent with the feminist politics of the time, Lepore reduces their relationship choices to Marston's psychology, thereby casting him as a deviant, a pervert, and a self-serving, controlling husband and father. In order to reach this conclusion, she ignores the political commitments to non-monogamy circulating at the time, as well as the interests of career women. In other words, Lepore's mononormative inability to see poly kinship obscures sociological explanations for and political implications of the relationship choices made by all three.

Given Lepore's presumption of gender exploitation in the Marston family, I have to wonder if the intersection of gender and mononormativity (men want multiple partners; women are exploited in polygamy) has rendered invisible more egalitarian forms of poly kinship that existed long before contemporary polyamory subcultures emerged. That is, perhaps the narrative about how contemporary polyamory is qualitatively different from the way people did poly relationships in the past is precisely because historians and biographers are unable to see non-monogamy as a personal *and* political choice. The political significance of poly relationships from the past is invisible when they are explained as individual and idiosyncratic choices rather than a political decision. In this way, it erases the politics of poly existence. This is particularly problematic when a rejection of monogamous marriage has been and continues to be a central, political agenda for all kinds of movements, like for instance, the anarchist movement led by Emma Goldman.

Love sick Emma Goldman and her jealous rage

Candace Falk's (1984) book, *Love, Anarchy, and Emma Goldman: A Biography* paints a portrait of the intimate life of Emma Goldman, an anarchist writer and activist who lived from 1869 to 1940. Falk is probably the world's foremost expert on Emma Goldman and has written several books about her. In *Love and Anarchy*, Falk focuses specifically on Goldman's personal life and intimate relationships. Because Goldman had an unwavering political commitment to "free love" and rejected the institution of monogamous marriage, *Love and Anarchy* is also a book about con-sensual non-monogamy, poly relationships, and the politics of gender and sexuality.

From the first page, Falk (1984) situates Goldman's rejection of monogamous marriage squarely in the context of her other political activities.

> [Emma Goldman] had advocated free love at a time when conventional mar-riage was the only norm and birth control when even literature on the subject was banned. She had fought for free speech when that right was often violated in practice and had agitated for the eight-hour workday when twelve hours was standard.
>
> *(1)*

Falk paints a compelling and sympathetic picture of Goldman's politics and personal life. However, the overarching narrative about consensual non-monogamy and poly relationships is that they are a "utopian" ideal and impossible to live up to in real life, and thus, despite her political rejection of monogamous marriage, Goldman was unable to live it in practice.

In order to make this implicit argument about non-monogamous relation-ships, Falk begins Goldman's story with her relationship with Ben Reitman rather than her life-long partnerships with Alexander Berkman ("Sasha") and Modesto Stein ("Fedya"). This is significant because Goldman's relationship with Reitman was more passionate, tumultuous, and painful than was her relationships with Sasha and Fedya. By beginning the story of Goldman's personal life with Reitman, Falk sets the tone for an over-emphasis on the emotional difficulty Goldman experienced in the non-monogamous relationship with Reitman on the one hand, and an underestimation of the support and life-long poly love and shared political commitments between her, Sasha, and Fedya.

As documented by Falk, the passion, jealousy, and insecurity Goldman felt in her relationship with Reitman was incompatible with her commitment to rational thinking, self-control, and free love. In other words, her public face was not her private experience. Falk (1984) writes:

> It was not just that Ben's sexual attraction threatened to overpower the strong, independent, rational woman, the feared and respected leader that the public Emma Goldman had become; to make matters worse, Ben continued throughout his relationship with Emma to live up to his repu-tation as a "lady's man." Although Emma was an outspoken advocate of free love and an opponent of marriage, she had to admit that Ben's fre-quent escapades "tear at my very vitals…turn me into something foreign to myself."
>
> *(4)*

Given the evidence provided by Falk, there is no doubt that Goldman was con-founded by these strong emotions in a world that constructed a strict binary between emotion and reason. However, at the same time, nowhere in Falk's evidence is there any indication that Goldman wanted to be in a monogamous, traditional marriage with Reitman.

In fact, the tumultuousness of the relationship seems less about jealousy and possessiveness, and more about Reitman's dishonesty and ambivalence toward Goldman's political goals. He stole money from Goldman's anarchist magazine, *Mother Earth*. He often had sex with women he met at the rallies at which Gold-man spoke and did not tell Goldman. If that were not enough, Goldman learned that it was Reitman who tipped off the police about Goldman's appearance at a rally in Chicago, which then led to her arrest. Despite these serious betrayals, Falk (1984) continues to pin Goldman's disappointment in Reitman on jealous rage and insecurity.

> Emma, the crusader for those impoverished by a capitalist system, could rationalize his stealing, even though it was reprehensible, but how could he squander and debase her love, when love was the most precious resource in the world? Of course she had had inklings of Ben's unfaithfulness before; she had watched "his bedroom eyes" flash across crowded rooms and even knew about one of his affairs. But his flirtations had seemed a harmless expression of his charm. Now Emma felt completely betrayed and confused. How could she have been so blind?
>
> *(59)*

Falk can't imagine that it was *lying* about his affairs, not sex with other women that was so hurtful, and that the relationship ended because Reitman sabotaged Goldman's career. From a poly perspective, it appears that Reitman was incapable of being ethical in any aspect of their relationship, including non-monogamy, and Goldman struggled with her overwhelming sexual attraction to him despite his duplicity. Goldman did not want monogamy; Goldman wanted a partner she could trust and with whom she shared political commitments—all of which it appears, she had with Fedya and Sasha.

Falk's emphasis on Goldman's relationship with Reitman rather than the one she had with Fedya and Sasha is puzzling given the duration and nature of her commitments to these life-long friends and on again/off again lovers. Before she ever met Reitman, Goldman lived with and was lovers with both Sasha and Fedya. Falk (1984) writes of that time "[Sasha and Fedya] lived compatibly together and enjoyed the warmth generated by this new 'chosen family' they had created with Emma. For the first time in her life, Emma felt really loved and genuinely happy" (21). The three of them pledged a commitment grounded in their shared political agenda as well as a deep affection and love for each other.

> Their loose *ménage a trois* reinforced by this solemn pledge, the three young idealists felt they could meet any challenge with the strength of their commitment and the knowledge that they were not alone. Fedya preferred to remain in the background, to express his dedication to his friends and to the cause through his art rather than through direct propaganda. Yet he was determined to live with Emma and Sasha as part of a communal economic, as well as political, unit.
>
> *(Falk 1984: 23)*

Falk tips her mononormative hand when she uses of the words "loose" and "idealists" to describe their relationship. Whatever Emma, Fedya, and Sasha were doing, according to Falk it was inevitably temporary and grounded in unrealistic idealism. From a poly perspective, however, poly households might not fit into normative ideas of what a stable family looks like, but that does not mean that they are any more temporary than other kinds of households.

Because Goldman never expressed the sort of sexual passion for Fedya and Sasha that she did for Ben Reithman, Falk is unable to see their continued commitment to each other as real or significant because the relationship was not always full of sexual passion and romantic feelings. Falk articulates and reinforces what Elisabeth Brake (2012) calls *amatonormativity*, which refers to "a focus on marital and amorous love relationships as special sites of value" and depends upon "the assumption that a central, exclusive, amorous relationship is normal for humans, in that it is a universally shared goal, and that such a relationship is normative, in the sense that it should be aimed at in preference to other relationship types" (5). All of the evidence provided by Falk quite convincingly shows that sexual passion was the defining feature of the relationship between Goldman and Reitman, but also that Goldman could not depend on him. The evidence also shows, however, that sexual passion diminished and eventually disappeared in Gold-man's relationships with Fedya and Sasha, but she maintained her affection, political ties, and mutual interdependence with them throughout her entire life.

As anyone who has been in a consensually non-monogamous or poly rela-tionship knows, there is a rather significant difference between *giving in to* feelings of jealousy and demanding monogamy on the one hand, and trying to understand and *overcome* those feelings on the other. Falk assumes that Gold-man's sexual passion and jealousy were incompatible with a commitment to free love. Surely, Falk shows quite clearly that Goldman struggled with her passion and jealousy. However, from a poly point of view, she did so precisely *because* she wanted to maintain a non-monogamous relationship with Reitman, which she did until the relationship ended. Moreover, with a poly gaze I see Goldman's poly relationship with Fedya and Sasha as evidence that, not only is it *possible* to live according to one's ideals of free love, Emma Goldman appears to have done so.

Finally, Falk suggests that Goldman's decision to not include the details of her relationship with Reitman in her memoir, *Living My Life*, was because she did not want to reveal the conflict between her political commitments to free love on the one hand, and the passion, possessiveness, and jealousy she experienced with Reitman, on the other. Like Lepore, Falk understates the very real negative social consequences that can be leveled against people practicing consensual non-monogamy in a mononormative world, especially for women. In fact, Falk (1984) concedes that a major reason that Goldman did not include the details of her relationship with Reitman in her memoire was because she believed exclud-ing the details of her unconventional sex life "might somehow help her to regain her citizenship" (5). Falk (1984) explains that Goldman "also feared that a book written without any self-censorship might not be accepted for publication, or, perhaps worse, would be viewed as sensational, obscuring everything that she had to say" (5). Quoting Goldman, Falk (1984) writes, "We all have something to hide. Nor is it cowardice which makes us shrink from turning ourselves inside out. It is more the dread that people do not understand, that what may mean something vital to you, to them is a thing to be spat upon" (8). And still, Falk (1984) attributes the exclusion to embarrassment over not being able to live up to her ideals.

> In the end, it was easier for Emma to criticize Ben than to face the questions that their relationships raised about the viability of her own dreams and expectations, when translated from abstract political principles into real life.
>
> Emma's early writings, speeches, and lectures centered on a vision of a total, liberating transformation in every realm of human life. Her dreams had not materialized, and the writing of the autobiography was a lonely coming to terms with a long series of disappointments. Her many political defeats, however, had never succeeded in destroying her spirit.
>
> (7)

Emma Goldman was jailed and eventually exiled from the United States for her political activities and beliefs. She also struggled with living a poly life in a mononormative world. Most relationships end, whether monogamous or poly, and thus the nature of her relationship with Reitman is but just one "disappointment." Still, Falk (1984) writes, "One part of her would have abandoned all her political work for a moment of sexual ecstasy with Ben. It was that uncontrolled aspect of her that she kept secret" (63). This is an oversimplification of the complications of living a poly life in a mononormative world, being an anarchist in a repressive political climate, and realizing that one's dreams had not been realized and never would be, and I believe, a disservice to the relationships she held outside of the one with Reitman.

Moreover, suggesting Goldman would give up everything for an elusive and ambivalent relationship with a man is not only inaccurate, it is also a deeply gendered narrative about what women want. Leaping to the mononormative conclusion that Goldman really wanted monogamy with Reitman, a "lady's man" incapable of monogamy, Falk reproduces the hegemonic narrative that men desire sexual novelty and women desire commitment. Goldman never did sacrifice her politics for a relationship with a man. As we learn later in *Love and Anarchy*, Goldman's comrades disapproved of her relationship with Reitman because of his duplicity and less-than-radical political commitments. Still, Falk (1984) continuously attributes Goldman's conflicting feelings for Reitman to his sexual relationships with others. Goldman's "embarrassment...at the disparity between her life and her ideals" (5) was not just about feeling jealous and possessive of Reitman; it was at least as much, if not more so, about how her passion for him led her, for a time, to overlook *his* failures to live up to her desire for an egalitarian, mutually respectful and committed partnership with someone she could trust and shared her political goals, which is exactly the relationship she had with Fedya and Sasha.

Susan Cheever (2014) makes similar mononormative assumptions in her biography of poet and life-long non-monogamist, E.E. Cummings. However, according to Cheever, E.E. Cummings was not so much a domineering pervert like William Marston, nor was he torn asunder by emotions like Emma Goldman. Instead, Cheever paints a portrait of E.E. Cummings as an immature, passive, self-indulgent man who was unable to "settle down" into an adult relationship with one woman and embrace the good provider role.

The immature, unreliable, and passive E.E. Cummings

Cheever's (2014) book, *E.E. Cummings: A Life*, provides a detailed account of E.E. Cummings' life, including his early involvement with the counter-cultural, and bohemian, early twentieth-century Greenwich Village. According to Cheever (2014), this was a "hobohemian lifestyle (including lots of drinking and sex), and the thrilling prospect of a new way of seeing the world, a new way of painting, and, especially, a new way of writing" (71). In this urban counter-culture, monogamy was rejected and, for this reason, Cheever writes, it was "just another utopian community."

> Greenwich Village in the 1920's was, in its own way, just another utopian community within the confines of an urban neighborhood. Cummings [was] not alone in believing that the human soul—if left unencumbered—could grow and create beyond all previous accomplishments. Like [other utopian experiments committed to non-monogamy]…Cummings and his fellow writers and the community they drew around them seemed to believe that, free from the ancient social institutions that had bound them and their parents, human beings would thrive.
>
> *(Cheever 2014: 80)*

Cheever reveals her underlying, mononormative assumptions by dismissing an anti-monogamy counter-culture as "just another utopian community" bound to fail because monogamous marriage is an "ancient social institution." This framing by Cheever also renders Cummings' commitment to non-monogamy, in particular a psychological desire to separate from his family of origin, especially his father.

Much of Cheever's narrative about non-monogamy revolves around Cummings relationship with Elaine and Scofield Thayer. Elaine and Scofield were married, and Cummings developed a close friendship with both. There is every indication that Cummings was sexually attracted to men and women, and that his close friendship with Scofield Thayer was not platonic.

> Cummings's life, as he wrote in his journals, had already been upended by the influence of Scofield Thayer—dapper, sophisticated, feminine, very rich, and on his way to Vienna to be psycholanalyzed by none other than Sigmund Freud…If it was Scofield Thayer who had enabled Cummings to break with his parents…then it was the fragile Elaine who would wean Cummings away from her husband. Freud himself, Cummings wrote, had urged Thayer to make Cummings marry Elaine.
>
> *(Cheever 2014: 73)*

Emphasizing a need to break from his parents, Cheever casts a sort of adolescent shadow on Cummings' relationship with Scofield, even suggesting that Elaine "weaned" Cummings away from him. Immediately following the reference to Elaine pulling Cummings away from Scofield, Cheever states that "none other than" Sigmund Freud endorsed a separation between the two bisexual men. It is difficult not to read this as an indication that not just Freud, but also Cheever, perceives Scofield and Cummings' relationship as unhealthy or unnatural.

Cheever seems a bit confounded by the whole situation and can't help sticking her proverbial tongue-in-cheek when referring to the counter-culture in which Cummings, Scofield, and Elaine were embedded.

So when the sexually confused Cummings and the sexually rejected Elaine both found themselves in Greenwich Village and within a few blocks from each other, the girl who Cummings had written "would make any man faint with happiness" and the witty young poet were suddenly free to be friends and even more than friends….Sex was meant to be free, everyone said. And as Cummings's friend Dos Passos wrote, "Those of us who weren't in love with Cummings were in love with Elaine."

(Cheever 2014: 74)

Cheever (2014) refers to Cummings as "sexually confused" (74) and Elaine as sexually rejected by Scofield, dismissing Cummings' and Scofield's bisexuality. It is apparently unimaginable to Cheever that forming a triad would make perfect sense to all involved. Casting Cheever's biphobia and mononormativity aside, from a poly perspective, it is entirely possible (likely?) that Elaine was not a wedge, but instead a conduit to Cummings and Scofield's relationship. As reported by Cheever (2014), while Thayer was in Vienna, he sent money back to Cummings so that he could take care of Elaine (74), and Cummings had written poems that were "fantasies of sex between Thayer and Elaine" (73).

Cheever's interpretation of the poly relationship as adolescent and unhealthy becomes even more evident when she describes how everything changed when Elaine became pregnant with Cummings' child.

Then, disaster. In May of 1919 Elaine told Cummings that she was pregnant with his child. It was one thing to be free, gloriously free, about sex and love and art. It was quite another thing to contemplate taking on the financial and emotional burdens of a child. How could he continue to work as an artist and as a poet if he was saddled with a family? Cummings balked. He urged Elaine to have an abortion. Thayer also urged her to have an operation to terminate her pregnancy…But Elaine, until now so delicate and pliable, decided that she wanted to have the child. For once in her life she would not be bullied by men.

(Cheever 2014: 76)

It is difficult not to draw a parallel between how Lepore assumed that Holloway and Byrne were victims of William Marston's selfish proclivities and Cheever's reference to Elaine as "delicate and pliable" and as having been "bullied by men." Cheever (2014) can't help but cast Elaine as a victim.

She was only nineteen when she first met Thayer; and the dramatic and painful few years of her marriage, her time as Cummings's mistress, and now the birth of her child may well have wounded her in ways that are hard to measure.

(77)

As I described above about Lepore and Terry Gross's discussion of Olive Byrne, the word "mistress" once again emerges rendering the couple primary and relationships outside of the dyad as intrusive infidelity. Cheever (2014) doesn't present any concrete evidence that Elaine's life during that time was "dramatic and painful" nor could she know if or how she was "wounded." Further, she attributes to Cummings and Scofield a desire to be "gloriously free, about sex and love and art" and to avoid taking on adult responsibilities. Not only is this pronatalist and heteronormative by equating adult responsibilities with taking on the "financial and emotional burdens of a child," it negates the possibility that, given the situation—Elaine and Scofield legally married and Elaine pregnant with Cummings' child—Cummings and Scofield might have other or additional reasons for not wanting Elaine to carry the pregnancy to term. Of course, there is no way of knowing for sure what motivated the men to discourage Elaine from having Cummings' child or for Elaine's decision to do so. Still, Cheever draws conclusions about motivations and emotional states based on hetero- and mononormative assumptions. Given our inability to really know whether or not one, both, or neither explanation is accurate, my critique of Cheever's confidence in her mononormative and heteronormative conclusions and her inability to entertain other, more poly possibilities, is not about arguing that I am correct and Cheever is wrong. Instead, my critique is meant to point to how the biography, as written, reproduces hegemonic ideas about family, gender, and adult maturity and about what constitutes a moral and "good life."

By the end of the biography, a poly reading of how the threesome dealt with the birth of the child might not be as far-fetched as Cheever might want. After Elaine gave birth to Cummings' daughter Nancy, Thayer adopted the child, and Cummings lived with them on and off for some time (Cheever 2014: 76). As was the case with the Marstons, discussed above, it seems to me that the poly arrangement was a solution rather than a problem in need of remedy. Still, Cheever can't help inserting her skepticism about the poly arrangement.

> On the surface, Cummings, Thayer, and Elaine were a highly civilized threesome dedicated to personal freedom and the idea that creative work had to come before personal lives. Still, Cummings couldn't help crowing over the adorable, tiny daughter who was finally put in his arms when she was a bit more than a month old...Before Nancy turned a year old, her parents seemed to have come back together in a permanent reunion—although of course the idea of anything permanent was anathema to them and to their community.
>
> *(Cheever 2014: 77)*

There is a strange presumption that a commitment to non-monogamy, creative work, and personal freedom as an alternative to conventional careers and marriage is somehow anathema to "anything permanent." About the four of them (including the child) living together, Cheever (2014) writes, "Cummings slept apart from the married couple. What kind of man was he then?" (76). As I have suggested elsewhere (Schippers 2016), this slight to Cummings' masculinity is part and parcel to mononormative and gendered discourses that emasculate men who "allow" other men to have intimate relationships with "their" women.

Despite the relative success of the poly arrangement, Cheever can't imagine that it could work, especially for Elaine.

> Over the next four years all would be buffeted about by their own feelings; Cummings was still in love with Elaine and would soon love the child she was carrying. Thayer himself was still attached to Elaine and might also have been a little bit in love with Cummings. Cummings himself had once had *that* (It. in original) crush on [the man] Sibley Watson. Elaine was naturally terrified, as most mothers-to-be are, and couldn't see herself finding safety with any of the alternatives available to her. For the moment, though the façade of principle was intact. Soon enough it would come dreadfully undone.
>
> *(Cheever 2014: 76)*

There is a confusion to Cheever's understanding of who is in love with whom and a disturbing reference that points to Cummings' bisexuality as a reason for Elaine's terror. Cheever's confusion, it seems, is grounded in a deeply mononormative and biphobic assumption that people cannot love and form bonds with more than one person and of different genders, and Cheever frames it as (inevitably?) a "façade" that would become "dreadfully undone."

Dreadfully undone begins with Elaine and Scofield's divorce, followed by Cummings' move to Europe in order to finish a book. However, as Cheever (2014) describes, Elaine and Nancy joined him in Paris less than a month later, "almost as if they had been part of a more conventional kind of family." Cheever continues: "With Paris in the background, Elaine and Cummings seemed to fall in love all over again. Paris allowed them to retain their fantasies of who they were" (78). Cheever's language consistently portrays them as never quite being a "real" family but instead merely "playing" family (78), as an "experiment" (79) and thus, as unstable and impermanent. When Elaine and Cummings married in March 1924, Cheever writes:

> Marriage didn't change much, and both promised that they would immediately release the other if that was wanted…By April the three were so much a family that Cummings even legally adopted his own child. Was this altogether too much bourgeois claptrap?
>
> *(Cheever 2014: 79)*

This last sentence sets up the end of the marriage as Cummings' failure because of his political commitments and his inability to play the conventional husband.

Cummings' supposed inability or unwillingness to be a good husband is a running theme of Cheever's contempt for him. For instance, when Elaine's sister died from pneumonia, Cheever (2014) writes:

An old-fashioned husband would have been on hand to help with the legal and emotional complications of such an intimate loss...Cummings, however, was the new kind of husband, and he hardly paid attention. Cummings may have had an idée fixe on right and wrong, but when it came to managing the adult world with all its aggravations and necessities, he was useless.

(80)

When Elaine fell in love with another man, Frank MacDermot, and MacDermot insisted that Elaine cut off her relationship with Cummings, Cheever (2014) writes,

[I]t's easy to guess why she was overwhelmingly attracted to a man like Mac-Dermot, the son of a self-made man, who had been attorney general for a British-ruled Ireland. MacDermot didn't have time for poetry and jokes and the vicissitudes of the creative life. For him, life was serious, and he was seriously in love with Elaine. For Cummings, nothing was serious—or at least that was the myth he had lived by.

(81)

According to Cheever, it came undone when, *over several years*, Scofield and Elaine divorced, Cummings and Elaine married and maintained their commitment to sexual freedom, and, eventually, Elaine fell in love with another man and ended her relationship with Cummings. In the long trajectory of their lives, relationships started and ended, as is the case in most people's lives. Cheever (2014), however, ties their doomed future to the futility of consensual non-monogamy: "They loved each other, and they left each other free—that was the idea. It's an idea that has cropped up in human history; an idea that rarely works out, especially when there are children involved" (79).

If we view this trajectory with a poly gaze, however, Elaine, Scofield, and Cummings, like Emma, Sasha, and Fedya, were, for a time, successful in forging a poly relationship. Moreover, once Scofield was out of the picture, Elaine and Cummings maintained a consensually non-monogamous relationship for several years. It is the case, apparently, that Elaine's relationship with MacDermot led to the demise of their marriage. Rather than seeing this as a failure of non-monogamy, however, one could interpret the end of the marriage as a reflection of mononormativity—after all, it was MacDermot who demanded Elaine cut off all ties to Cummings. In the end, if one is committed to free love and not to the ties of monogamous marriage, separation and divorce is painful, but it is not necessarily a failure of non-monogamy. Perhaps the poly relationship between Cummings, Scofield and Elaine came "dreadfully undone," not because they, and Cummings especially, were anti-monogamy. Perhaps, instead, it is more because of the pervasiveness of compulsory monogamy. Of Elaine, Cummings said, "I didn't want to possess her...I wanted: to do as she liked, to please her" (Cheever 2014: 75). Though certainly heartbroken, it appears that Cummings, like Emma Goldman, lived according to his principles, despite the overwhelming cultural reach of mononormativity.

Writing poly lives as political

Not all biographers adopt a mononormative lens through which they interpret poly lives. For instance, unlike Lepore, Falk, and Cheever, Alexis De Veaux's (2006) *Warrior Poet: A Biography of Audre Lorde* situates Lorde's ideological commitment to non-monogamy squarely within the broader context of her political life. Rather than reading Lorde's poly relationships as dissonant with her political ideals, De Veaux (2006) interprets them as an articulation of those ideals.

> Lorde wanted to believe in, and practice, loving without boundaries—a philosophy and behavior she found consistent with rebellion against heterosexually scripted models of monogamy. Her choice represented the uncharted landscape, the "new nameless country," of loving women without becoming imprisoned by those very models…she was free then to be sexual with whomever she wanted, whenever she wanted. She began to experiment with having one loving relationship with a specific partner, and separating that relationship from sexual intimacy with friends.
>
> *(57)*

Like Goldman and Cummings, Lorde was embedded within a politicized counterculture that rejected conventional marriage. Unlike Falk and Cheever, however, De Veaux (2006) casts the rejection of monogamous marriage in positive terms and as consistent with other political goals.

> They shared a dream of the country's political possibilities and experimented with visions of a new social order—one beyond racial and sexual boundaries. They became an extended family. Within the group, the lines between heterosexual, homosexuality, bisexuality, love, and friendship blurred. Irrespective of gender, sex between the friends was no secret…Lorde was the only black female in the group, the only avowed lesbian, a poet, and single. She exploited the control that being single and desired afforded, managing a flow of friends who were lovers to her Mount Vernon apartment.
>
> *(69)*

Eventually, however, as De Veaux (2006) describes, Lorde "began to tire of having lovers she slept with and then sent home to someone else…she felt lonely and wanted a primary partner of her own" (72). By saying Lorde desired a primary partner *rather than* suggesting she wanted a monogamous relationship, De Veaux demonstrates an awareness of the difference.

When Lorde decided she wanted a primary partner, Edwin Ashley Rollins, a gay, white man came into her life. De Veaux (2006) explains their attraction to each other as grounded in a mutual rejection of conventional marriage and commitment to doing kinship differently.

> From the start, Audre and Ed made known to each other their same-sex
> desires. As their courtship evolved, they also came to understand that neither
> was interested in a conventional marriage, though both believed in the con-
> ventions of marriage and that they could raise children in a new kind of
> family. They were idealists, rebelling against mainstream norms.
>
> *(74)*

Like the other biographers, De Veaux (2006) casts them as idealists, but situates
their idealism within broader identity politics of the time.

> Though they were of dichotomous worlds as black and white, and subaltern
> cultures as lesbian and gay, America was in the throes of social transformation;
> they had at their fingertips the possibility of creating a new kind of marriage.
>
> *(76)*

Lorde and Rollins married and had children together, but throughout the marriage Lorde maintained emotionally and sexually intimate relationships with
women and Ed pursued sexual relationships with men. De Veaux (2006) describes
the marriage as difficult and "at most obvious…a social experiment." In De
Veaux's telling, however, it was not the relationships they had with others outside
of the marriage that made it difficult.

> Beneath the skin, the marriage broiled with slow-cooking problems that
> seeped out and surfaced. Audre knew little about living with a man as Ed
> knew about living with a woman. She was dominant and authoritative. He
> was submissive enough, but he had an orthodox sense of his role as provider,
> [quoting Lorde] "an image of what he thought the perfect husband was and
> he tried to be it." He doted on her…But Audre demanded that Ed be
> emotionally responsive.
>
> *(78)*

Unlike Cheever's description of Cummings' inability to be a good provider, De
Veaux describes Rollins' efforts to *be* the good provider as the problem for it did
not fit into Lorde's feminist commitment to "a new kind of family."

In addition, De Veaux (2006) suggests that the relationship ended because of
Ed's inability to accept and be open about his desire for men, and this chafed
against Lorde's anti-heteronormative politics and her commitment to sexual
liberation.

> According to Lorde, Ed became more secretive than ever about his outside
> sexual life. That their own sexual life was sporadic and he was sexually
> engaged with men was not the issue to Lorde. The issue was dishonesty and
> denial. Ed would be gone for hours on one pretext or another, and she
> instinctively felt he was out picking up men. When he came back, she'd ask

him what he'd been doing. Ed would refuse to talk, avoiding her interroga-tions as to why he didn't bring his lovers home, as she did, and be up front about whom he was with.

(88)

This is a stark contrast to how Falk characterizes the difficulty Goldman experi-enced in her relationship with Reitman. Nowhere in this poly narrative about Lorde's relationship to Rollins does De Veaux question the consistency between Lorde's political ideals and the way she lived her life. Nor does she belittle or render ridiculous Lorde's life-long commitment to the erotic, non-monogamy, and forming intimate relationships with others.

Like De Veaux, Nancy Milford (2002) paints a positive and loving portrait of a life of non-monogamy in her biography of Edna St. Vincent Millay, *Savage Beauty: The Life of Edna St. Vincent Millay*. Millay was a contemporary of Cummings in Greenwich Village and, like Cummings, embraced non-monogamy as a political and personal imperative. In fact, in her biography of Cummings, Susan Cheever (2014) sets up the "hobohemian lifestyle including lots of drinking and sex" by offering this brief and somewhat off-hand comment about Millay:

Edmund Wilson and John Peale Bishop were both hopelessly in love with Edna St. Vincent Millay. When she decided to sleep with them simulta-neously, all of them remembered, there were heated discussions about who would get the top of her and who the bottom.

(72)

Unlike Cheever, however, Milford (2002) does not snicker at the ridiculousness of the Greenwich Village counter-culture and its anti-monogamy commitments. Instead, she situates Millay's interest in sex and non-monogamy squarely in another aspect of Greenwich Village, that being changing gender norms and more freedom for women. For instance, She writes,

The Scrappy young women and men, often living together just a few blocks shy of the Italian families to the south, came from another America, and not just for cheap rents and free love…Uptown men wore suits with vests and high starched collars, and women wore corsts. In the Village, men wore cor-duroy shirts and tied their neckties around their waists as belts. Greenwich Village women smoked and didn't wear corsets, and as Art Young, the bril-liant cartoonist for the Masses, wrote, "Here a woman could say damn right out loud and still be respected."

(Milford 2002: 163)

It is in this context—feminism and careerism, that Milford (2002) situates Millay's rejection of monogamous marriage.

> To [Millay] the Freudian program required woman's complete sexual surrender to man—which might be inevitable but which brought an inescapable penalty; for when a girl gave herself completely to her lover, he would soon stop being in love with her—and then she could pine for him forlornly or turn lightly to another lover.
>
> *(156)*

Milford describes Millay as unwilling to form permanent relationships with men and as flirtatious, coy, and irresistible. At the same time, she does not interpret these as character flaws. Instead, Milford contextualizes them in Millay's desire for the freedom to explore her sexuality and focus on her work.

> Millay was not unaware that certain men in her life, particularly the literary men who would later leave written records...found her refusal to continue her affairs with them a stunning rejection. They wrote to her about their desperate hurt and anger; they waylaid her on the street. To a man they felt that her leaving them meant far more about her inability to be faithful than it did about their need to secure her exclusively for themselves. They talked about her chagrin, even when it was clearly their own; they talked about her promiscuity and her puzzling magnanimity. They failed to acknowledge the pull she felt between the excitement and energy of her sexual life, where she was a sort of brigand who relished the chase, and the difficult, sweet pleasures of her work.
>
> *(205)*

Millay eventually married Eugen Boissevain, a self-proclaimed feminist and widower of suffragist Inez Milholland. They remained together for the rest of their lives and, significantly, they both continued to have other lovers throughout their marriage. Like the others discussed above, Edna St. Vincent Millay, apparently, was successful in living up to her ideals and lived a poly life.

Conclusion

There is a larger story here when we consider all of these biographies together. The mononormative narratives about the Marstons, Goldman, and Cummings draw on and implicitly endorsed links between mononormativity, heteronormativity, and gender relations. All three biographers frame their narratives about consensual non-monogamy and poly kinship through a deeply Western notion of normal family relations and the "good life." In all three books, the poly lives of Marston, Goldman, and Cummings are read as a selfish peculiarity, a failure to live up to utopian ideals, and an excuse to avoid adult responsibilities. In addition, each of these biographers uses a gender lens to evaluate their subjects. We have Marston, the self-serving, domineering, and duplicitous polygamist; Emma Goldman, the hopeless romantic who desperately wanted but never had family; and E.E.

Cummings, an irresponsible and immature man who refused to take on the good provider role. With these gendered narratives, they render poly kinships invisible and rejections of monogamous marriage a personal choice or failure rather than grounded in political commitments.

Having said this, I want to establish that my goal in this chapter is not necessarily to criticize Lepore, Falk, and Cheever, but instead to draw attention to their inability to adopt a poly gaze. Because mononormativity is rather ubiquitous, and polyamory is a relatively new concept, there is no reason to expect biographers to be aware of their own mononormativity.

However, at the same time, monogamy is privileged, and consensual non-monogamies and poly relationships have been and continue to be marginalized and stigmatized. That the authors never considered an alternative reading of these poly lives reflects their monogamy privilege. Just as anyone who writes about disadvantaged groups from a position of race, class, gender, or sexual privilege must tread lightly, acknowledge the limits of their understanding, and check their privilege, so must those who are privileged by *relationship status*. As the biographies written by De Veaux and Milford suggest, it is possible to write non-monogamy and poly lives differently and with more understanding and respect. Checking monogamy privilege or writing biographies with a poly gaze might go a long way in terms of acknowledging poly lives from the past, not as pathological, utopian, or impossible endeavors, but instead as political and personal successes.

Finally, narratives that portray poly relationships and commitments to non-monogamy from the past as utopian but doomed experiments perpetuate the false assumption that there is something exceptional about contemporary polyamory. Erasing the political motivations of poly figures from the past occludes similarities between what we are doing now and what has been done in the past. Perhaps contemporary polyamory is not so different after all, and history is not a path of progression and things "getting better." Without placing a poly gaze on these and many others who have, in the near and distant past, embraced non-monogamy and poly relationships as a personal *and political* commitment, it will be difficult to, as Przybylo and Cooper (2014) demand, recognize how resonances from the past can inform our identities and politics in the present.

References

Brake, Elisabeth. 2012. *Minimizing Marriage: Marriage, Morality, and the Law*. New York: Oxford.

Cheever, Susan. 2014. *E.E. Cummings: A Life*. New York: Vintage Books.

De Veaux, Alexis. 2006. *Warrior Poet: A Biography of Audre Lorde*. New York: Norton.

Falk, Candace. 1984. *Love, Anarchy, and Emma Goldman: A Biography*. New Brunswick: Rutgers University Press.

Lepore, Jill. 2014. *The Secret History of Wonder Woman*. New York: Vintage Books.

Milford, Nancy. 2002. *Savage Beauty: The Life of Edna St. Vincent Millay*. New York: Random House.

National Public Radio (NPR). 2017. "The Man Behind Wonder Woman Was Inspired by Both Suffragists and Centerfolds." June 9, 2017. Originally broadcast October 27, 2014. https://www.npr.org/2017/06/09/532149100/the-man-behind-wonder-woman-was-inspired-by-both-suffragists-and-centerfolds?t=1563454554577.

Pallotta-Chiarolli, Maria. 2010. *Border Sexualities, Border Families in Schools.* New York: Rowman & Littlefield.

Przybylo, Ela and Danielle Cooper. 2014. "Asexual Resonances: Tracing a Queerly Asexual Archive." *GLQ: A Journal of Lesbian and Gay Studies* 20(3): 297–318.

Schippers, Mimi. 2016. *Beyond Monogamy: Polyamory and The Future of Polyqueer Sexualities.* New York: New York University Press.

Sheff, Elisabeth. 2014. *The Polyamorists Next Door: Inside Multiple-Partner Relationships and Families.* Lanham, MD: Rowman and Littlefield.

Willey, Angela. 2016. *Undoing Monogamy: The Politics of Science and the Possibilities of Biology.* Durham, NC: Duke University Press.

5

POLY-POSITIVE NARRATIVES AND AMERICAN SEXUAL EXCEPTIONALISM

Introduction

Thus far, I have adopted a poly gaze to interpret mononormative narratives about historical figures from the past (Chapter 3) and polygamy (Chapter 2). In both cases, I suggested that, as authors marginalize or pathologize poly lives, they often articulate already circulating discourses about gender, sexuality, race, and nation. In the remaining chapters, I turn my gaze to narratives about poly lives that render poly relationships possible, if not desirable. I ask the same questions running throughout the book. What are these stories saying about poly relationships and, in these representations of poly lives, what are the implicit messages about gender, sexuality, race, and nation? Who is portrayed as happy and deserving of a "good life," and who is rendered undeserving?

In this chapter, then, I adopt a poly gaze to take a closer look at two films, *Savages* and *Splendor*. Although very different kinds of films, one a violent, action drama and the other a romantic comedy, both feature relatively positive representations of polyamorous relationships. My focus, however, is not to determine whether or not polyamory is represented in "accurate" or sympathetic ways—in both cases, the films are poly positive. Instead, my goal is to peel back the initial pleasure in being hailed by poly-positive narrative and analyze what, in their representations of polyamory specifically, they say about what constitutes "happiness" and a "good life" and about *who* deserves a good life and the rights of citizenship.

In *Beyond Monogamy* (Schippers 2016), I argued that, as polyamory emerges as an increasingly viable and visible relationship style, it is important to distinguish between polynormative and polyqueer representations of polyamory. As discussed in previous chapters, polynormativity is a term that refers to poly practices, beliefs, and norms that most closely resemble white, gender conforming, class privileged heteronormativity. Polynormativity includes a set of moral imperatives about the best and most ethical way to do polyamory. These moral guidelines are sometimes offered up by polyamorists as evidence that polyamorists and poly families are just like "normal" families except that there are more than two adults. The problem with aspiring to be normal and policing others to conform, of course, is that it reproduces already existing systems of privilege and disadvantage, and those who choose to live differently from the norm are cast as undeserving (Warner 1999). Polyqueer relationships or subcultures are distinguished from polynormative ones in that norms, beliefs, and practices within a subculture or relationship reject heteronormativity and challenge or flatten race, ethnic, gender, and class hierarchies.

A poly gaze, then, would include paying close attention to how narrative efforts to normalize polyamory implicitly or explicitly produce moral standards for how to live "the good life" and establish boundaries around who is deserving of happiness and the rights of citizenship and who is not. My goal is to demonstrate, by way of example with these two poly positive films, how a poly gaze opens analytic space to move beyond the pleasure of being hailed by poly narrative and asks important sociological questions about what sort of cultural work these representations do beyond normalizing or sensationalizing polyamory. What we shall see is that, in both films, the poly positive content is embedded within a broader, implicit message about American sexual exceptionalism (Puar 2007). They are, I will argue, exemplary of American *poly* exceptionalism.

American poly exceptionalism

In her book, *Terrorist Assemblages: Homonationalism in Queer Times*, Jasbir Puar (2007) argues that contemporary discourse about gay and lesbian rights in the United States is characterized by what she calls *American sexual exceptionalism*. American sexual exceptionalism refers to a network of ideological discourses that define the United States as exceptionally progressive, tolerant, and protective of sexual minorities. One way the United States is constructed as exceptionally sexually progressive is by constructing other nations or cultures as exceptionally less tolerant or repressive. For instance, in order to define the United States as sexually exceptional, media representations of the "The Muslim Terrorist" construct a caricature of Islam as homophobic and sexually repressed and fundamentally different from the "liberated" gay or lesbian U.S. citizen (Puar 2007). According to Puar (2007), "a more pernicious inhabitation of homosexual sexual exceptionalism occurs through stagings of U.S. nationalism via a praxis of sexual othering, one that exceptionalizes the identities of U.S. homosexualities vis-à-vis Orientalist constructions of 'Muslim sexuality'" (4). The social construction of the "free" gay or lesbian U.S. citizen casts the United States as exceptionally tolerant and democratic by constructing others as exceptionally intolerant and oppressive.

Building on Puar's general concept of American sexual exceptionalism, I define American poly exceptionalism as the social construction of contemporary U.S.

culture as exceptionally tolerant of polyamory and of American polyamorists as exceptionally progressive, gender egalitarian, and sexually appealing. For example, I ended Chapter 3 by suggesting that contemporary constructions of polyamory as gender egalitarian, enlightened, and progressive often depend upon drawing distinctions between polyamory and Mormon or Muslim polygamy. American poly exceptionalism is nested within and bolsters U.S. nationalism by sexually othering un-American Mormon and Muslim Fundamentalists. It "exceptionalizes" the identities of U.S. polyamorists vis-à-vis Orientalist constructions of Muslim polygamists and constructions of Mormon fundamentalists as un-American.

To further develop American poly exceptionalism as an analytic lens with which to unpack other kinds of poly-positive narrative, below I adopt a poly gaze to reveal an underlying and pernicious American poly exceptionalism in the films *Savages* (Stone 2012) and *Splendor* (Araki 1999).

American poly exceptionalism in the film *Savages*

Savages is a film written and directed by Oliver Stone and released in 2012. The main plot revolves around two American drug dealers in a violent and deadly rivalry with Mexican drug cartel. As Kathleen Staudt (2014) suggests, the film is very much about the geographical and cultural "borderlands" between the United States and Mexico.

> On each side of the border, by each group of drug dealers, the perception exists of the "others" as savages. Amid the sunshine of the Pacific coastal beaches, luxury homes, and sailboats, filmmakers use excessive blood and violence that ultimately portray Mexicans as more violent...US savagery seems more "civilized"...Ultimately, the film polarizes the border, but with more sophisticated guise. The film *Savages* maintains the pattern whereby contemporary US films otherize Mexico.
>
> *(474)*

Staudt emphasizes how a hierarchical border between the ostensibly superior Americans and abject Mexicans is established through the portrayal of Mexicans as more savage than Americans. Building on her work, I turn my poly gaze to how representations of the American characters' polyamorous relationship punctuate the border itself and articulate already circulating racist and xenophobic constructions of exceptional and deserving Americans and abject, undeserving Mexicans.

The film begins with the character and voice-over narrator, Ophelia, played by the blond, blue-eyed Blake Lively, inviting the audience to witness her story. Ophelia begins, "Let's get back to where it started. Here in paradise. Where they say God parked himself on the seventh day and got towed on the eighth." Several short vignettes of beach life in Laguna Beach, California are followed by an aerial shot of cliff-top mansions overlooking the ocean. As the camera zooms in to enter one of the homes, Ophelia says, "And this is Ben and Chon's hole in the wall by the sea. Paid for in cash. Not bad for two Laguna dudes who are definitely not employable on Wall Street."

Inside the doorway, we find Ophelia having sex with her lover, Chon, played by the white, muscular, and tattooed Taylor Kitsch. Ophelia continues,

> Chon is a killer. 2 tours in Iraq …and he came back with a lot of cash, but no soul. He's always trying to fuck the war out of himself. I have orgasms. He has wargasms. So I guess I try to give him back some of the things he's lost. Chon is the love of my life.

In a post-coital glow, Ophelia lights a joint while Chon checks an incoming email message. The message contains a video of severed heads and decapitated bodies and a demand to meet. When Ophelia asks if it's Iraq, Chon replies, "No, Mexico." According to Ophelia's narration, the reason for the threatening video is "because Ben and Chon grow some of the best weed in the world." In the first few minutes of the film, the audience is introduced to the wealthy, sexy Americans living in paradise. And Mexicans are threatening to come in and take all of it, including their lives.

We are then introduced to Ben played by Aaron Taylor-Johnson. When he arrives at the same mansion in a black limousine, Ophelia runs and jumps into his arms. He, too, is young and white, but, unlike Chon, he is lean and sporting long dreadlocks that have been bleached by the sun. While we watch Ophelia and Ben "make love," Ophelia narrates his introduction,

> This is Ben. The other love of my life…I know what you're thinking. Slut. Right? Maybe it is wrong, but the truth is, we all love each other so much. We trust each other. We take care of each other. And for me, they are one complete man. Chon is cold metal. Ben is warm wood. Chon fucks. Ben makes love. Chon is earth and Ben spirit. And the one thing they have in common is me. I'm the home that neither of them ever had. And they're mine.

The combination of O's narration and the intimacy between the three of them makes it abundantly clear that this relationship is polyamorous. Ophelia is in love and sexually involved with both men, and although Ben and Chon are not lovers, they are "best friends since high school." Their business endeavor is criminal, but the wealth they have accumulated by growing "the best" marijuana in the world paints the characters with just enough individualistic, entrepreneurial, and rebel spirit to contextualize and explain their unconventional poly relationship and to render them as sexy, poly Americans.

Surely, this is a representation of a rather *polynormative* relationship—they are young, white, beautiful, and wealthy. At the same time, however, there is something unusual about Ben and Chon's willingness to love the same woman. The

FIGURE 5.1 Ophelia, Ben, and Chon share an intimate embrace after an erotic threesome
Source: *Savages* 2012.

men's bond is both economic (they run the marijuana business together) and sexual (they are both in love with Ophelia). In fact, there is a scene in which Ben, Chon, and Ophelia enjoy a sexually intimate threesome. Though Chon does not explicitly "fuck the war out of himself" with Ben's body, and we do not witness Ben "making love" with Chon, the scene depicts a deep intimacy between all three including a post-coital cluster cuddle.

Ben and Chon share what I call polyqueer, homosocial bonds (Schippers 2016). They do not compete with each other to possess Ophelia. Instead, they agree to be *metamours*[1] in their mutual love for her. In the first ten minutes of the film, we get a rather positive, albeit polynormative representation of the poly relationship; they are privileged, young, and beautiful, they love and trust each other, and they seem to have a stable, American, poly household. In the first scenes described above, it appears as if their relationship just happens to be polyamorous, and polyamory is not driving the plot as a conflict in need of resolution.

However, as the film continues, it become clear that the poly configuration of their relationship is necessary for the plot *and* for punctuating their American exceptionalism. As we shall see below, the polyamorous structure of the relationship forges a bond between Chon and Ben that is at once familial (they are both "married" to Ophelia) but not based on blood. Because they "share" Ophelia and work together to protect her from the Mexican drug cartel, as the plot unfolds, Ben and Chon are rendered "brothers" in citizenship and in their shared and mutual claim to sexual ownership of and need to protect white womanhood.

In order to render the Americans as exceptionally deserving of their marijuana business, their upper class economic standing, and their claim to "home," including the U.S. side of the border and the lovely Ophelia, the film juxtaposes the Americans as exceptionally civilized against Mexican men as exceptionally brutal. For instance, during an initial conversation between Ben and Chon about how to deal with the threats, Ben suggests they hand over the business and walk away. Chon replies, "You don't get it Ben. It's a jungle thing. When they smell your fear, they like it. They will attack us. They're fucking savages." Chon's language to describe the Mexicans—"Smelling fear," "a jungle thing," "they will attack," and "they are savages"—equate Mexican masculinities with animalistic savagery. In another scene, Dennis, an FBI agent on the take and working for Chon and Ben, played by John Travolta, also uses animalistic language to refer to the Mexicans. As he, Ben, and Chon discuss the impending attempt by the Mexican Drug Cartel to steal the business, Ophelia is conspicuously absent, marking her as less a business partner and more an object shared between the men. Dennis warns them not to challenge the "hostile take-over."

> They're killing each other down Mexico way. That's why they're moving north. The forks are out. The pie's getting smaller...We used to keep the animals in the zoo, but now with this war on drugs it's like the war in Iraq... take the deal instead of decapitation. Keep banging that sweet California ass.

This contrast between the invading Mexicans and their predilection for decapitation on the one hand, and Ben and Chon living the good life by "banging that sweet California ass" on the other, is a not-so-subtle statement about sexuality, the good life, and entitlement to white womanhood.

The rivalry between the supposedly deserving Americans and the invading Mexicans who threaten their way of life is an old trope about the United States, Mexico, and immigration (Chavez 2013). Xenophobic and racist imagery portray undocumented immigrants as a dangerous and undeserving population that threatens the safety and economic security of "deserving" Americans. In his book *The Latino Threat: Constructing Immigrants, Citizens, and the Nation*, Leo Chavez (2013) suggests that mainstream discourse in the United States constructs a Mexican abject Other who is assumed to be ready to pour over the U.S./Mexico border and threaten the American way of life.

> [Mexican immigrants'] social identity has been plagued by the mark of illegality, which in much public discourse means they are criminals and thus illegitimate members of society undeserving of social benefits, including citizenship. Latinos are an alleged threat because of this history and social identity, which supposedly make their integration difficult and imbue them, particularly Mexicans, with a desire to remain socially apart as they prepare for a reconquest of the U.S. Southwest.
>
> *(4)*

In the film *Savages*, polyamory is the vehicle through which Ben and Chon are bound together as Americans on one side of the border while the Mexican drug cartel threaten to cross and take over their "territory," which includes their successful business and their woman, Ophelia. It is significant that, throughout the entire film, only Ben and Chon discuss what they should do about the threat. Ophelia is either absent during these discussions or remains passive as they tell her what they are going to do. While their polyamorous relationship seems relatively egalitarian, when it comes to the real business of commerce and war, her only function as a poly partner is to forge a familial-citizen bond between the men.

This American, familial, but sexually progressive poly bond is punctuated when we meet their nemesis, Lado, played by a disheveled and mustachioed Benicio Del Toro. In the introductory scene, Lado and his "crew" are disguised as landscapers and arrive in a beat-up pickup truck at the home of a lawyer who failed to adequately represent a Mexican drug kingpin. Mexican mariachi music plays as they proceed to terrorize and ultimately kill the lawyer and his girlfriend. The explicitly violent and drawn-out assassinations establish Lado as ruthless and capable of brutal violence.

However, and importantly, Lado's brutality is also sexual. After murdering the lawyer, Lado instructs his associate, Estoban, played by Diego Cataño, to kill the lawyer's girlfriend. When Estoban hesitates, Lado offers the woman to him by asking, "You want to fuck her?" While leaning in to the young man's ear and demanding he pull the trigger, Lado inserts a finger into the woman's vagina. After Estoban kills her, Lado sniffs his finger. Lado is not just a killer; he's also a rapist. Women are objects that he can offer to other men or take himself without consent.

This scene creates a cultural and gendered border between Lado's treatment of women and Ben and Chon's pampering of Ophelia and willingness to "share" her with each other. Unlike the violent rape scene in which Lado offers the woman to Estoban and where it is clear that the woman is an insignificant object, the

FIGURE 5.2 Disguised as a landscaping crew, Lado arrives with his men to execute a
    disloyal business partner
Source: *Savages* 2012.

polyamorous character of the relationship between Ben, Chon, and Ophelia appears to be loving and kind and masks her function as an object to foment the bond between the men. By rendering Ben and Chon as polyamorous, the film constructs the Americans as exceptionally, sexually progressive and egalitarian and the Mexicans as exceptionally sexually violent and misogynistic.

Lado's treatment of women comes through in another scene when he is with his wife. They are in the bleachers watching their son play a Little League baseball game. Lado yells at and threatens his son to play better. He also describes his daughter as "look[ing] like a whore" and at risk of getting "knocked up." Angrily, he says to his wife, "We should sit down at the table. The whole goddamn family, 'cause I can see what's happening." Lado's character is written as having one foot in mainstream American culture (baseball, daughter adopts American fashion and looks like a slut, they don't eat dinner together), but at the same time as not fitting in and longing to go back to a more traditional way of life.

When Lado's wife reminds him that they immigrated to the United States to escape that kind of traditionalism, Lado suggests they go back to Mexico. She tells him not to embarrass her in public and to shower when he returns from his mistress. Aggressively, Lado grabs her by the arms and threatens that she should be careful and remember her place. The narrative contrast between Lado's adultery on the one hand and the poly relationship shared by the Americans on the other emphasizes the *sexual differences* between the Americans and the Mexicans and renders the Americans as exceptionally progressive and egalitarian and the Mexicans as patriarchal, controlling, and duplicitously unfaithful.

In another scene, Lado and Estoban watch Ophelia, Ben, and Chon return one evening to their mansion. Undetected, Lado and Estoban watch from their beat-up pickup truck as, obviously drunk and playful, Chon lifts Ophelia out of their sports car and carries her to the house. When he stumbles, he hands her over to Ben. Lado asks, "So which cock does she suck?" Estoban replies, "Can't tell. White guys like each other. Maybe they're faggots," to which Lado says, "Maybe she does them both. Savages." This is now the third time that the titular word "savages" appears in the script. Unlike when Chon and Dennis use the word to describe violence, Lado uses the label to refer to Ben and Chon's sexual identities and practices. Lado and Estoban perceive the Americans as uncivilized because Ben and Chon might be "faggots" and Ophelia a slut. The audience knows that Ben and Chon are not lovers, and in the first scene Ophelia puts to rest the idea that she is a slut by saying they love and trust each other. Unlike the sexually progressive American characters (and audience?), Lado and Estoban are old-fashioned, if not sexual bigots. They cannot see polyamory, nor how egalitarian, progressive, and free the Americans are.

Once the symbolic sexual "border" between the Americans and Mexicans is established, Lado's boss, the Mexican drug "Queenpin" Elana, played by Selma Hayek, arranges to have Ophelia kidnapped and held by Lado until Ben and Chon surrender the business. The rest of the film involves the Americans trying to get Ophelia back. As they do so, they use a military-grade arsenal and enlist

Chon's marine comrades to exact extremely brutal violence in their war against the invading Mexicans. At this point in the narrative, however, the savagery Ben and Chon inflict on others is constructed as a response to the savagery of the Mexicans.

There is only one other time in the film when the titular word "savages" is used. It is the final scene, and once again Ophelia is offering voice-over narration as she strolls along a tropical beach.

> I'm not sure there could ever be three people equally in love. It just doesn't work that way. I looked up the definition of savage. It means cruel, crippled, regressed back to a primal state of being. One day, maybe, we'll be back. For now, we live like Savages. Beautiful savages.

The beach setting suggests that they were able to escape both the cartel and federal prosecution by following through with a plan set earlier and before Ophelia was kidnapped. The destination was Indonesia where, according to Ben there is "a pretty little village. I put in a water system. Near the beach," and it is populated by "the sweetest people you'd ever want to meet."

It is ironic that "beautiful savages" becomes a label Ophelia uses for herself and her lovers, for throughout the film it had been hurled across the cultural borders between the Americans and the Mexicans as an epithet. Perhaps it makes sense given the definition she provides. Certainly Chon and Ben were "cruel." No doubt they were all "crippled" by the entire ordeal, and now settled into a small Indonesian town, "regressed back to a primal state of being." Their savagery is narrated as provoked and temporary. Given their American poly exceptionalism—wealthy, white, beautiful, and sexually progressive—the audience is encouraged to see their savagery as provoked and thus necessary and temporary. At their core, despite the violence, they are beautiful, American savages.

In the end, no matter how critical Oliver Stone might have intended to be about the indulgences and colonial sense of entitlement characteristic of Americans, his rendering of gender, sexuality, and ethnicity establishes a different kind of border. It is one that, through poly narrative, puts the exceptionally sexy, progressive, and egalitarian Americans on one side and the exceptionally violent, homophobic, and misogynistic Mexicans on the other. It is tempting to be hailed by and simply enjoy a rare depiction of a polyamorous relationship. However, when viewed with a poly gaze and with attention to what the film is saying about ethnicity, citizenship, and sexuality, it becomes clear that it reinforces and articulates rather racist and xenophobic American poly exceptionalism.

Poly-positive narratives do not have to depict such explicitly violent, racist, and xenophobic imagery in order to establish American poly exceptionalism. In fact, a more subtle form of American poly exceptionalism can be tucked into light-hearted, romantic comedies. Such is the case with the film *Splendor*. *Splendor* is not a violent, action-filled drama or about the serious business of violently protecting ethnic, national, and cultural borders. Instead, it paints a portrait of polyamory as fun, humorous, and edgy, but ultimately as an exceptionally progressive, urban, and enlightened path to settling down into adulthood and finding happiness by creating an exceptional American family.

American poly exceptionalism in *Splendor*

Splendor is a romantic comedy in which Veronica, played by Kathleen Robertson, falls in love with two men at the same time. Like *Savages*, the film begins with Veronica's voiceover: "Love is a mysterious and baffling thing." While the opening credits roll, we see a beautiful, young, blond woman in a threesome with two men, also young and beautiful, one blonde, the other brunette. The woman turns to the brunette and says, "Love you, Abel." Abel (Johnathon Schaech) says, "Love you, V" (short for Veronica). She then turns to the blonde man, "Love you, Zed." Zed (Matt Keeslar) replies, "Love you Ron" (also short for Veronica).

The voiceover then becomes a documentary style interview scene. Veronica faces the camera and the audience and begins to explain.

> No. This is not a dream sequence. I was raised in your basic strip mall heaven where dreams are limited to either an exciting career as a beautician or marrying some guy with "From Beer to Eternity" tattooed on his bicep. My dreams were too big for suburbia, so I decided to move to LA and do something really different.

In this first segment, Veronica establishes herself as someone who could never settle for her suburban hometown with its strip malls and limited career choices and marriage options. Veronica is the kind of woman who dreams of something bigger. Her American dream can only be found in a big city where she can do something "really different." That something different, it turns out, is a polyamorous relationship with Zed and Abel, the blonde and brunette with whom Veronica is having a threesome during the opening credits.

Veronica meets Abel and Zed one night while she and her best friend, a punk, lesbian, artist named Mike (Kelly MacDonald) attend a Halloween costume party. Veronica encounters Abel who is costumed as Prince Charming. They don't have much time to chat because Mike drags Veronica away toward the stage where a band is about to play. Mike is hot for the woman bass player and wants a better view. As Veronica and Mike walk away, Prince Charming raises his costume sword and yells, "I am Abel!" The double meaning of his name is a joke, but within the context of the opening threesome scene, it also foreshadows his ability to be Veronica's poly mate.

As the band begins, Veronica's eyes fall on the blonde, muscular drummer who turns out to be Zed. Wanting to meet the bass player, Mike brings Veronica back stage. It is there that Veronica literally bumps into Zed. Unlike the brief encounter with Prince Charming interrupted by Mike, Zed and Veronica find themselves alone and, without exchanging names, jump each other's bones in a fevered sexual romp.

Veronica explains in voiceover:

> My mom raised me to be a more polite, reserved type. But with Zed, let's just say I was more outgoing than usual. I guess all those years of being a good girl finally got to me. I mean I came to the city to cut loose although I was thinking more along the lines of not paying off my student loans than doing it with some stranger on the floor of a public toilet.

With her mother now standing in to represent her suburban and conservative past, Veronica claims her urban, progressive, and outgoing place in the world. Tired of being a "good girl," Veronica becomes "outgoing" by having casual sex with a stranger. On her way out of the club, she once again runs into Abel. Despite Mike's protestations and disgust at the heteronormativity of it all, Veronica gives Abel her phone number.

In the next scene, Veronica is waking up in her own bed with Zed, who is sporting a large erection, creating a comedic tent in the sheets. While Veronica and Zed have sex again, Abel calls and begins leaving a message on her answering machine. Abel says that meeting Veronica was "like déjà vu only with a person instead of a place." As Zed and Veronica simultaneously orgasm, Abel's voice on the answering machine fills the room. Veronica explains to the audience that what she has with Zed could be "something major." However, she "couldn't get Prince Charming out of [her] brain." She continues, "I figured if things with Zed didn't work out, it wouldn't hurt to have a back up."

Describing her desire to date both men to Mike, Veronica's main interlocutor when she is not engaging the audience directly, Veronica worries that her conscience won't allow her to mislead them. Mike replies, "Your conscience is a bit over developed for a 22 year old." Mike, Veronica's lesbian, best gal-pal is there throughout the film to counsel the decidedly straight Veronica. However, Mike's presence in the narrative is more than to serve as interlocutor; it is also a way to render Veronica's character as exceptionally tolerant of queerness and to set the stage for her openness to bucking the norms of monogamy.

Still struggling with the ethics of dating two men, Veronica decides to go on a date with Abel in hopes that she won't be attracted to him, can forget about him, and focus fully on Zed. Instead, she finds that Abel is "sweet" and "sexy," and she is strongly drawn to him. In a voiceover, Veronica struggles with her conscience and says, "Abel is thinking I am totally this innocent girl next door while upstairs my toothbrush is still wet from Zed borrowing it."

She decides that she likes Abel too much to not tell him the truth. After inviting him into her apartment, she tells him about Zed. At first Abel is chagrined and can't believe he's "being shafted for a drummer." Veronica tells Abel that she feels a connection to him, and Abel asks, "And the drummer?" She says, "The same." Abel quietly says, "Some guys are emotionally equipped for handling a situation

FIGURE 5.3 Veronica is consoled by her best friend, Mike
Source: *Splendor* 1999.

like this. I, unfortunately, am not one of those guys." Veronica quickly says, "I'm not one of those girls either." Abel decides he should leave, but cannot stay away. When he returns to her door, he says, "Let's just go with the flow and see what happens." They fall into each other's arms and Abel spends the night.

We then see Veronica telling Zed about Abel. Zed says that he has done the "dating other people thing," but that this "feels different." Veronica agrees that it is "definitely different." Zed agrees to give it a try saying, "Whatever happens, happens. He sounds like a wimp anyway." In this sequence, Veronica goes from concern over the ethics of dating two men at the same time to being an "ethical slut" (Easton and Hardy 2009). Rather than lying to or deceiving them, Veronica is totally honest and up front with Zed and Abel, and, much to her surprise, they agree to give it a try. Veronica initially keeps them separate because each expresses extreme jealousy about the other, but the idea of them accidentally running into each other is exciting because of "the danger of it."

Eventually, the two men accidentally meet. When they realize who the other is, without any discussion or verbal exchange, they immediately get into a physical fight. To deal with the situation, Veronica invites them over to dinner the next night hoping that, "If Abel and Zed could become friends they wouldn't be so jealous of each other." After dinner and many alcoholic beverages, she suggests they play Truth or Dare. When she dares Abel to kiss Zed, he balks. Disappointed, Veronica says, "It would be so hot. You're totally turning me off right now." Not wanting to turn her off, Abel kisses Zed on the cheek. Veronica then dares Zed to kiss Abel "full on the lips." The two men begin kissing, and eventually, with Veronica between them, embrace and have a threesome. In voiceover, Veronica explains, "Seeing the two of them together made me realize this is an opportunity

to do something really different. Something I never could have done back home."
Again Veronica invokes her past and "back home." It is not just Veronica who is
sexually progressive and open. Apparently Zed and Abel are also down with doing
something "really different."

When Veronica tells Mike about the encounter, Mike is shocked. No longer
representing queerness, Mike becomes a conservative, mononormative voice. She
asks Veronica if she realizes that her life has turned into a *Three's Company*
episode.[2] Veronica replies that she thought the show was "pretty progressive for its
time." In her pursuit of polyamory, Veronica is portrayed as more enlightened than
her lesbian best friend, and progressive polyamory is the evidence.

The men, too, are exceptionally progressive. For instance, when Zed loses his
job, he moves in with Veronica. Abel is jealous and explains to Veronica, "Look.
This is not acceptable, okay? The three of us can have sex together. We can sleep
in the same bed. People can think we're deviant freaks. I don't care. But I am not
cool with Zed moving in like this." The solution is not to kick Zed out, but
instead to invite Abel in and live as, in Veronica's words, "one happy, kooky,
family." Solidifying the positive and progressive rendering of polyamory, Veronica says, "As demented as our relationship seemed to the outside world, it
worked. It was like the rules that apply to everyone else didn't apply to us. Life
was good."

Then Veronica meets another man, Ernest (Eric Mabius) who, as Veronica
explains to Mike, is "reliable," "doesn't collect action figures," and "picks up the
check for dinner." Mike asks her, "Can you imagine being 80 years old and still
having three-ways?" Veronica winces, "Ew." Still the voice of mononormativity,

FIGURE 5.4 Veronica, Zed, and Abel try something "different" and are blissfully happy
       as a triad
Source: *Splendor* 1999.

Mike warns her, "Forget Ernest. You, my lady, are already one boyfriend over the legal limit." Mike continues to be the voice of conservative mononormativity.

The stability of the happy, kooky family is put to the test when Veronica discovers she is pregnant. Before telling Zed and Abel, we see her at what is obviously a need-the-money, odd job. Sporting a red, white, and blue sequined jump suit and a frown, she holds a tray of finger food at an auto show. A Musak version of the song *America the Beautiful* plays in the background as random men wander by and take morsels from her tray. Experiencing morning sickness, she throws up into an American Flag napkin and runs to the bathroom. Two women in the same sequined outfits come in and, not realizing Veronica is in the stall, one tells the other that she heard Veronica lives with two guys and they all "fuck each other... Isn't it disgusting. Those nice girl types are always the biggest sluts." Significantly, the two women are less attractive than Veronica, and they have 1960s' bouffant hairdos. As they talk about her, the camera is on Veronica's tear-streaked face encouraging the audience to feel empathy for her. Unlike Mike's friendly but sometimes chastising take on being "really different," the women's comments in the bathroom are old-fashioned and bigoted, and it appears that Veronica takes them to heart.

Feeling overwhelmed, Veronica returns to the apartment she shares with Zed and Abel and tells them she needs space for a few days. While staying with Mike, Zed and Abel call continuously. Zed informs her that he has gotten a job, and Abel tells her that they bought a Christmas tree and would like to decorate it together with her. In these conversations, Abel and Zed use "we" language to talk about how much they miss her. The men want their poly family back, but Veronica feels she needs to be responsible because of the baby.

At this time, Ernest, who is class-privileged and seeking a heteronormative, monogamous relationship swoops in and offers to take care of her. He invites her to take a weekend vacation at his condo in Maui. Disturbed by the idea of Veronica cheating on Zed and Abel, Mike insists she decline. Despite this, Veronica is compelled by Ernest's maturity and economic security and goes to Maui anyway. Veronica explains to the audience why.

> It was like I was trying so hard to escape from my small town past that I hadn't stopped to think about the future. I was terrified of ending up like my mom struggling alone with a baby if Abel and Zed flaked on me. Ernest on the other hand was definitely the kind of guy that would stick around whether it was fun or not.

Veronica struggles with her "small town past," but this time it is not about career options and husband prospects; it is about being a single mother and economically deprived. She decides be "responsible" by breaking up with Zed and Abel and choosing Ernest. As she explains, Ernest makes her feel "Safe enough to finally make the decision to keep my baby." Ernest proposes marriage by saying "I want your baby to have a real mother and father," and unable to resist the offer of secure heteronormativity, Veronica accepts. They are to be married two weeks later on New Year's Eve.

Mike is apoplectic about Veronica "ball and chaining [herself] to someone [she doesn't] even love." Given the choice between monogamous, loveless heteronormativity on the one hand and polyamory on the other, even Mike is on board with the latter.

It is New Year's Eve, and as Zed and Abel commiserate and console each other about losing Veronica, Veronica prepares for her wedding ceremony. After Veronica confesses to Mike that it is the worst day of her life, Mike fully embraces polyamory by phoning Zed and Abel to let them know Veronica is marrying Ernest and pleads with them to come rescue her.

Frantically, Zed and Abel assist each other in cleaning themselves up and make their way to the hotel where the wedding is taking place. After Mike gives them the keycard to Veronica's room, they burst in and find that she is not there. Moving to the balcony, they see her below. The wedding is taking place by a pool, and Veronica is walking up the aisle toward Ernest. Confused, Veronica looks up at them and asks them what they are doing while Ernest encourages someone to call the police.

Wanting to rescue Veronica, Zed executes a super-hero leap from the balcony into the pool. Although Abel initially decides to take the safer route by heading to the stairs, he changes his mind and, like Zed, successfully executes the super-human leap to the pool. Together, they hold on to each other to stay afloat. Zed tells her that he has gotten a real job at Guitar Center, and Abel informs her that he will finally finish his novel. The leap into the pool was not just an effort to rescue Veronica; it was a leap into mature adulthood and a willingness to do the right thing. Presenting an ultimatum, Abel says, "Him or us. Once and for all and we'll leave you alone." Before Veronica can answer, the screen fades to pink.

When an image again appears, we see Veronica standing over a crib and staring down at twins. Abel and Zed come up to stand on either side of her. As the three of them gaze at the babies, Abel says, "They got my eyes." Zed adds, "My mouth." Smiling, Veronica corrects them. "Boys, you're both wrong. They look exactly like I did when I was a baby." Abel asks, "So are we ever gonna know who the father is?" Zed says, "They're mine, aren't they?" Abel scoffs, "In your dreams, Bozo. One hundred percent mine, right V?" Veronica smiles and replies, "They're ours."

All three smile and again look at the babies. Abel and Zed kiss Veronica on the cheek and, as the credits roll, we can assume they live happily-ever-after as a happy, kooky, and polyamorous family.

From a poly perspective, this film is, in every way, a poly-positive narrative. Rather than ending with monogamous coupling, happily-ever-after is found through polyamory. There is something decidedly queer about pregnancy suturing two masculine competitors into a polyamorous relationship with the same woman. It is, if nothing else, a counter-narrative to the idea that men are naturally

FIGURE 5.5 A happy, polynormative, ending. Veronica, Zed, and Abel gaze lovingly at
the twins
Source: *Splendor* 1999.

possessive, jealous, and violently controlling *because* they want to ensure offspring
are theirs. In the closing scene of *Splendor,* *not* knowing the paternity of the twins
makes family possible. Furthermore, it is a relatively rare, light-hearted, and
humorous representation of polyamory as fun, progressive, and possible. However,
if we look deeper with a poly gaze, we can once again see polyamory standing in
as American sexual exceptionalism.

Like in the film *Savages*, the characters are young, white, conventionally
attractive, and exceptionally sexually tolerant. They live in the urban setting of
Los Angeles, and, in the case of Veronica, needed to leave behind small-town
conservatism to fully embrace progressive polyamory. This mirrors what Jack
Halberstam (2005) refers to as "metronormativity," in LGBTQ narratives of
coming out.

> This term reveals the conflation of "urban" and "visible" in many nor-
> malizing narratives of gay/lesbian subjectivities. Such narratives tell of clo-
> seted subjects who "come out" into an urban setting, which in turn
> supposedly allow for the full expression for the sexual self...the metro-
> normative narrative maps a story of migration onto the coming out narra-
> tive...the metronormative story of migration from "country" to "town" is
> a spatial narrative within which the subject moves to a place of tolerance
> after enduring a life in a place of suspicion, persecution, and secrecy. Since
> each narrative bears the same structure, it is easy to equate the physical
> journey from small town to big city with the psychological journey from
> closet case to out and proud.
>
> *(36–37)*

Splendor spins a metronormative narrative about the spatial possibilities of poly-amory. Over and over, Veronica narrates the city of Los Angeles as the "place" where doing something "different" becomes possible—where being polyamorous is possible. Significantly, the fictional "small town" from which she came represents both mononormativity and gender conformity, and both must be surpassed in order to be polyamorous. Also, by conflating the stated conservativism of the small town with the chastising voice of Veronica's mother, the small town stands in for compulsory gendered sexuality and a requirement to be a "good girl," meaning sexually restrained and monogamous. Veronica's metronormative spatial story punctuates the narrative insistence that polyamory is inherently a more enlightened, progressive, and gender egalitarian path to happiness.

In addition, the presence of Mike as the best friend but also the voice of mononormativity displaces lesbians (or other queers), as the path to finding happi-ness beyond heteronormativity. As a lesbian, Mike punctuates Veronica's sexual tolerance, but, at the same time, she has no sexual desire or erotic life and, sig-nificantly, she has no lesbian friends or any ties to a lesbian community or sub-culture. Her life revolves around either chastising the very straight Veronica or facilitating heterosexual polyamory. She is the quintessential "gay best friend," and she has two functions. One is to shine a light on the heterosexual characters' exceptionally progressive and enlightened sexual attitudes, and the second is to articulate resistance to polyamory so the main characters can show how wrong she is. By isolating Mike from other lesbians and lesbian culture, the narrative hetero-sexualizes polyamory while completely ignoring or rendering invisible anti-monogamy politics in lesbian culture (Willey 2016). As the comedic sidekick, Mike's desires, politics, and sexual culture are absent, invisible, and thus completely irrelevant. To add heteronormative insult to injury, Mike's character growth is demonstrated by her eventual acceptance of heterosexual polyamory and by put-ting in motion Veronica's rescue from monogamous, heterosexual marriage, not by Mike herself, but by Zed and Abel. The lesbian sidekick puts in motion the pos-sibility of heterosexual polyamory *and* the very gendered dynamics of the men rescuing Veronica, the damsel in heteronormative distress. In the end, exception-ally progressive polyamory, not lesbian identity or culture, coalesces as the ultimate antidote and progressive alternative to heteronormativity.

And, ironically, Veronica's rejection of heteronormativity takes shape as a rather heteronormative version of family and happily-ever-after. The narrative conclusion and happy ending is polyamorous procreation. Veronica consistently refers to the "future" when struggling with the unwanted pregnancy. Her decision to "keep the baby" pushes her toward monogamous marriage, but in the end she and her babies are rescued by polyamory. When Zed and Abel step up and claim the provider role, and Veronica happily accepts their offer, the polyamorists are rendered mature and responsible. Adult responsibilities, maturity, and happiness are wrapped up in a baby blanket and reproduction. Though we have no idea how the polyamorous family fares in the future—in fact we can't know in order to maintain the illusion of polyamory as happily-ever-after—the closing image of the babies signifies a legitimate future for the polyamorous relationship among the adults. Halberstam (2005) refers to this as "reproductive time."

> [R]espectability, and notions of the normal on which it depends, may be upheld by a middle-class logic of reproductive temporality...in Western cultures, we chart the emergence of the adult from the dangerous and unruly period of adolescence as a desired process of maturation...Within the life cycle of the Western human subject, long periods of stability are considered to be desirable, and people who live in rapid bursts...are characterized as immature and even dangerous.
>
> *(4–5)*

The image of Veronica, Zed, and Abel (the now responsible adults) gazing at the twins signifies the men's trajectory from immature boys to mature adults, thus normalizing polyamory as consistent with these heteronormative, temporal trajectories. While this happy ending challenges the stereotype of polyamorists as harmful to children (Pallotta-Chiarolli 2010; Sheff 2014), it does so by presenting polyamory as consistent with rather than an alternative to the heteronormative, nuclear family.

Veronica, Zed, and Abel want to be happy, and, as narrated in the film, what will make them all happy is living in a progressive big city, loving each other, and raising their twins. They are a perfectly normal American family except for the small detail that there are three parents instead of two. Mike is no longer in the picture, and, thus, queerness recedes in the background. Veronica no longer is interested in a career or rejecting the role of "good girl." Being a good mother to her children is now the source of her happiness. In the end, poly love and babies are all she needs to live happily-ever-after. Although poly-positive, this narrative articulates a cruel optimism (Berlant 2011) lurking in discourses about polyamory as progressive, gender egalitarian, and normal. The film conveys a message that polyamory is exceptionally progressive and transgressive, but also the path to a good, mature, and reproductive life. And it does so by pushing queerness to the side and embracing heterosexual reproduction and a pronatalist version of what real family is.

Conclusion

In this chapter I adopted a poly gaze to identify how *Savages* and *Splendor* are poly-positive narratives, but also how they normalize polyamory by representing it as an example of American poly exceptionalism and as consistent with the perfect American family. These, of course, are not the only films (or other popular culture) that positively and sympathetically portray polyamory. As poly-positive stories emerge in popular culture, as they have in recent years, it is imperative that we pay close attention to what those narratives say about nation, ethnicity, race, gender, and sexuality. My analysis of these two films is just one example of how, and an invitation to others who take pleasure in positive representations of polyamory to look beyond the plea-sure of being hailed by poly-positive narratives and imagery and look deeper at what they are saying about who deserves happiness and what it means to live a good life.

While this chapter highlights who gets thrown under the bus in normalizing narrative about polyamorous relationships, in the next chapter I leave poly-normative narratives and adopt the poly gaze to peak under the bus and look for what might be left behind when representations of poly kinship jettison romantic, sexual relationships and heteronormative family as the road to happiness, the good life, and security.

Notes

1 The word "metamour" is the label polyamorists use to describe people who are partnered with the same person.
2 *Three's Company* is a 1970s' American television show in which a man and two women live together as roommates.

References

Araki, Gregg. 1999. *Splendor* [Film]. California: Samuel Goldwyn.

Berlant, Lauren. 2011. *Cruel Optimism*. Durham, NC: Duke University Press.

Chavez, Leo. 2013. *The Latino Threat: Constructing Immigrants, Citizens, and the Nation*, 2nd edn. Stanford, CA: Stanford University Press.

Easton, Dossie and Janet W. Hardy. 2009. *The Ethical Slut: A Practical Guide to Polyamory, Open Relationships, and Other Adventures*, 2nd edn. Berkeley, CA: Celestial Arts.

Halberstam, J. 2005. *In a Queer Time and Place: Transgender Bodies, Subcultural Lives*. New York: New York University Press.

Pallotta-Chiarolli, Maria. 2010. *Border Sexualities, Border Families in Schools*. New York: Rowman & Littlefield.

Puar, Jasbir. 2007. *Terrorist Assemblages: Homonationalism in Queer Times*. Durham, NC: Duke University Press.

Schippers, Mimi. 2016. *Beyond Monogamy: Polyamory and the Future of Polyqueer Sexualities*. New York: New York University Press.

Sheff, Elisabeth. 2014. *The Polyamorist Next Door: Inside Multiple-Partner Relationships and Families*. New York: Rowman and Littlefield.

Staudt, Kathleen. 2014. "The Border, Performed in Films Produced in Both Mexico and the US to 'Bring Out the Worst in a Country'." *Journal of Borderlands Studies* 29(4): 465–479.

Stone, Oliver. 2012. *Savages* [Film]. Los Angeles, CA: Universal Pictures.

Warner, Michael. 1999. *The Trouble with Normal: Sex, Politics, and the Ethics of Queer Life*. Boston, MA: Harvard University Press.

Willey, Angela. 2016. *Undoing Monogamy: The Politics of Science and the Possibilities of Biology*. Durham, NC: Duke University Press.

6

THE (POLY) LOVE THAT DARE NOT SPEAK ITS NAME

Poly kinship as a design for living queerly

Introduction

Can you think of a film or television show in which characters are coupled, if not married, or the plot is leading the characters toward "getting together"? Can you think of a film or television show you've watched in which the characters say that they are "in love" or "falling in love" and their love is expressed sexually? Of course anyone who has watched American film or television has witnessed these themes of sex, love, and marriage hundreds of times. In fact, given the ubiquity of romance (there is an entire genre devoted to it) in narrative visual media, it might make more sense to ask whether or not you can think of a film or a TV show that *does not* include characters in sexual love, coupled, and married or who are on their way to marriage. Even if the film is not about relationships, the sexual couple makes for a standard sub-plot or background story.

Now, think of a film and or a television show that features family, love, and commitment, and the characters refer to their relationships as polyamorous or poly? Although rare compared with narratives of coupling, there are some films (as described in the last chapter, for instance) and a few American television shows that feature polyamorous relationships, and some even use the word "polyamory" to describe these relationships. These would include, for instance, the reality television show *Polyamory: Married and Dating*, the web series *Unicornland*, and the Audience Network series *You, Me, Her*. In Spike Lee's Netflix series remake of *She's Gotta Have It*, the main character, Nola P. Darling, describes herself as a "fluid, polyamorous pansexual," and a character in the Netflix series *The Sinner* describes to police how two, shady characters presented themselves as "polyamorous" to lure her into a sexual relationship before fleeing her for her money.

The accuracy or sympathy with which media portray polyamorists is important, and I have no doubt that many researchers, media critics, and others are carefully parsing the content of these and other shows to assess what they say about polyamory. As I suggested in the conclusion of the last chapter, my hope is that others doing this work pay close attention to, not just what popular culture content says about polyamory and polyamorists, but also to what they convey and about whom in order to render polyamory possible and desirable. Because I have no doubt that many others are writing about media portrayals of polyamory, in this chapter I focus less on media texts that explicitly feature polyamory and polyamorists and instead turn the poly gaze onto narratives about poly relationships, kinship, and community in unexpected and unnamed places. Because they are not about polyamory as a sexual and romantic relationship and lovestyle (Anapol 2010) or a neoliberal choice for building the perfect American family, they might go unseen as poly narrative.

Specifically, I will adopt a poly gaze in order to "see" *queer* poly family, kinship, and community in the films *Shortbus* and *Cat Dancers* and the television show *Grace and Frankie*. I suggest that, because these films and this television show are not about sexual and romantic polyamory as a "legitimate" relationship or family choice, they do not fall into the heteronormative or polynormative traps outlined in the last chapter. Instead, they offer narratives of poly kinship that queer notions of family, kinship, and community by displacing rather than reproducing dominant cultural narratives that establish romantic and sexual coupling, dependent children, and extended blood kinship ties as the very definition of family and the only way to live a good, fulfilling, and secure life.

Coupling, heteronormative family ties, and the good life

Heteronormative prescriptions for how to live a good, fulfilling, and secure family life establish monogamous coupling and marriage as the first steps. Contemporary narratives about "good" marriages assume that sexual desire and romantic love are the initial impetus to "get together," and desire and love are the glue that binds individuals to each other (Coontz 2005). Sexual exclusivity is necessary in order to maintain family bonds over the life course (Kipnis 2003; Mint 2004), and relationship longevity is the mark of marital success (Halberstam 2005).

According to heteronormative logic, a heterosexual identity forecloses the pool of potential mates, and gender identity is the first and foremost criteria for choosing with whom to build a family. To the extent that narratives about "good marriages" (whether between same or other gendered partners) braid together erotic desire, monogamous coupling, and sexual identities, they are embedded within and support amatonormativity (Brake 2012), or the institutionalization and valorization of sexual, romantic relationships as a core feature of the social self and as more significant, enduring, and fulfilling than any other kinds of relationships. The monogamous and long-term aspects of "good" marriages, then, both reflect and perpetuate rather fixed notions of sexual identities.

Heterosexual identity and heterosexual behavior in the context of monogamous relationships are tied up with and, indeed, define what family and kinship is and should be. Institutionalized practices and ideological representations of the "good life" that neatly twine together monogamy, romantic love, sexual identity, family, and kinship into a normative whole are the foundation of heterosexual culture and belonging. Lauren Berlant and Michael Warner (1998) write:

> A complex cluster of sexual practices gets confused, in heterosexual culture, with the love plot of intimacy and familialism that signifies belonging to society in a deep and normal way. Community is imagined through scenes of intimacy, coupling, and kinship; a historical relation to futurity is restricted to generational narrative and reproduction.
>
> *(Berlant and Warner 1998: 554)*

Gendered, sexual desire and romantic love are the affective sutures to the entire social fabric, including family, kinship, community, and nation.

Couples become a "family" when they produce or adopt dependent children, and, in fact, the very definition of "family," in contemporary U.S. culture hinges on having kids. The questions, "Do you want to have a family some day?" or "When are you going to start a family?" are really questions about introducing dependent children into the couple relationship and household. The presence of children then, is evidence of one's commitment to "belonging" in the community and nation and to the future of the heteronormative family (Ahmed 2010). The heteronormative definition of kinship broadens the "family" temporally as in past and future generations, and it is circumscribed by past, present, and future blood or marital relationships that extend outside the nuclear family. Embedding this package into notions of security, Halberstam (2005) refers to this as inheritance time.

> The time of inheritance refers to an overview of generational time within which values, wealth, goods, and morals are passed through family tieds from one generation to the next. It also connects the family to the historical past of the nation, and glances ahead to connect the family to the future of both familial and national stability. In this category we can include the kinds of hypothetical temporality—the time of "what if"—that demands protection in the way of insurance policies, health care, and wills.
>
> *(5)*

Heterosexual coupling, having children, and maintaining extended kinship ties are key components to insurance, health, and inheritance key to a long, healthy, and happy life. because, it is presumed, our genetic, marital, and extended kin will provide emotional and physical support through the life course, and they will care for us in our old age.

As Sarah Ahmed (2010) suggests, narratives about "happy families" do not simply steer us toward particular kinds of family structures; they produce an affective investment in those structures. "We hear the term 'happy families' and we register the connection of these words in the familiarity of their affective resonance." Happy families, then, are far more than simply a set of relationships; they are "a promise, a hope, a dream; an aspiration." (45) Ahmed goes on to explain how narratives of happy families include affective investments in notions of community, kinship, and nation. "The happy family is both a myth of happiness, of where and how happiness takes place, and a powerful legislative device, a way of distributing time, energy, and resources. The family is also an inheritance. To inherit the family can be to acquire an orientation toward some things and not others as the cause of happiness. In other words, it is not just that groups cohere around [the happy family]; we are asked to reproduce what we inherit by being affected in the right way by the right things." (Ahmed 2010, 45) The hetero or homonormative ties that bind do not simply bind individuals together; they bind individuals to pursuing a kind of life that reproduces the self, the family, and the nation. This narrative is a powerful if not compulsory incentive to be affectively invested in and pursue family in order to live a happy, good, and moral life.

Media representations and narratives about coupling, marriage, and family as either the magical key to happiness or as taken-for-granted background, play a central role in heterosexual culture. With few exceptions, mainstream American television and film are a unified drumbeat marking the pace and direction for following the heteronormative path to happiness, safety, and security. However, as Halberstam (2005) suggests, a queer life is one that rejects the pace and direction of heteronormativity, and media texts that offer alternative narratives about with whom and how to form affective and familial ties are queer culture.

Queering the ties that bind through poly narrative

According to Berlant and Warner (1998),

> radical aspirations of queer culture building [is] not just a safe zone for queer sex but the changed possibilities of identity, intelligibility, publics, culture, and sex that appear when the heterosexual couple is no longer the referent or the privileged example of sexual culture.
>
> *(548)*

If queer culture dislodges the heterosexual couple as the privileged example of sexual culture, then queer world-making means forming relational connections through something (anything?) other than the heterosexual couple, dependent children, and extended kin. Unlike the normative heterosexual family script that dictates that a heterosexual identity leads to coupling with someone of the "opposite" sex, having children, and maintaining kinship ties with genetic or martial relatives, queer ties emerge in the *doing* rather than in the *being* family. When the heterosexual, monogamous couple is no longer the foundation of building familial ties, and one departs from the heteronormative path toward "happy families," then family formation becomes DIY (do-it-yourself) with the "do" being the operable term in this equation.[1] Whether or not those ties are queer is less a question of with whom, and more a question of *how* they are formed. Halberstam (2005) writes:

> Queer uses of time and space develop, at least in part, in opposition to the institutions of family, heterosexuality, and reproduction. They also develop according to other logics of location, movement, and identification. If we try to think about queerness as an outcome of strange temporalities, imaginative life schedules, and eccentric economic practices, we detach queerness from sexual identity and come closer to understanding Foucault's comment in "Friendship as a Way of Life" that "homosexuality threatens people as a 'way of life' rather than a way of having sex."
>
> *(1)*

Applied to media representations, then, narratives of familial or affective ties that reject heteronormative definitions of family and kinship would constitute queer world-making through narrative. For instance, building on the concept anti-monogamy (Rosa 1994), Angela Willey argues that Alison Bechdel's comic, *Dykes to Watch Out For* offers a representation of what Willey calls, dyke anti-monogamy. Dyke anti-monogamy is not the same thing as polyamory.

> Guides to and stories about polyamory offer us some models, but as they gain popularity in our (queer) communities, recipes for poly living are increasingly prescriptive and often couple-centric...Despite its linguistic formulation, anti-monogamy for Rosa is not the opposite of monogamy. It is not an alternate sexual subjectivity but rather "a way of life" oriented to undoing mono-gamy...Antimonogamy is...rather inspirational. Its ambitions stem from a rejection of certain tenets that would proscribe our relationships and define our desire in reductive ways: it suggests an ethic of destabilization.
>
> *(Willey 2016: 96)*

For Willey (2016), dyke antimonogamy is grounded in "friendship, community, and social justice," (97) and about Bechdel's comic strip in particular, Willey (2016) writes:

> Bechdel offers us a world in which monogamy is visible as a powerful social rule, a compelling cultural story, and a set of deeply embodied desires. In this world, dykes practice a way of life in which alternatives to monogamous coupling are considered as a matter of course and in which affective ties and networks of social support are not organized primarily around sex.
>
> *(101)*

According to Willey (2016), dyke antimonogamy also includes "friends and an extended family of exes with whom [one] shares various aspects of...life and on whom [one] relies for the companionship and support usually relegated exclusively to the locus of the couple" (107). Queer world-making within the context of dyke antimonogamy, then, includes de-centering sex as the organizing principle for forming affective ties *and* rejecting the notion that the couple is the only source for companionship and support.

Because one of the uses of the poly gaze is to "see" poly connections where they have not yet been recognized, it can be useful for finding representations of non-heteronormative or queer poly ties and connections. To illustrate this further, I now turn to three examples of media representations of poly ties that are something else altogether from heteronormative, homonormative, or polynormative[2] definitions of family and kinship.

Grace and Frankie: Poly affectivity as design for aging

Grace and Frankie is a Netflix series that centers on the lives of Grace, played by Jane Fonda, and Lily Tomlin's character, Frankie. The premise of the show is established in the first episode when their husbands, Robert played by Martin Sheen and Sol played by Sam Waterston, reveal that they, Robert and Sol, are gay, in love with each other, and want to get married. As Robert says to Grace in a very crowded restaurant and with Frankie and Sol at the table, "I'm leaving you." He then turns to Frankie and says, "And he's leaving you." Sol and Robert are divorce lawyers and have been partners for 30 years and, as revealed in the premier episode, have been secretly sexually involved for 20 years.

In the premier, Grace and Frankie's only tie is being the wives of law partners. The women can barely tolerate each other because they are so very different. Frankie is a pot-smoking, incense burning, left-leaning former hippie, and Grace is an upper class, designer-clothes-wearing, business entrepreneurial snob. Grace is uptight, drinks vodka martinis all day, and never eats bread or sauces. Frankie is an artist who burns sage and drinks peyote tea.

Despite their differences, upon learning that their husbands are leaving them to marry, Grace and Frankie begin to lean on each other. They first become roommates and best friends, but as the show progresses, they work with each other and with Sol and Robert to build a *poly affective family*. Elizabeth Sheff (2014) defines poly affective relationships as involving "people…who see each other as family members but are not sexually connected" (20).

Although Frankie and Grace are not lovers and neither are still sexually involved with their husbands, the relationship between the four of them is rendered as decidedly poly (but not polyamorous) in that they are inter-dependent, affectionate, and treat each other as family—much like what is expected of marital partners, adult children, or extended kin. For example, the poly affectivity between the formerly married and now divorced characters Frankie and Sol is captured during episode six in season one. There is an earthquake and, having an irrational fear of earthquakes, Frankie panics and climbs under the dining table in the home she shares with Grace. Not having lived with Frankie for very long,

Grace doesn't know what to do. She frantically offers Frankie different kinds of anti-anxiety medications, and when Frankie refuses, Grace grows increasingly frustrated and annoyed.

Meanwhile, Sol is in his home with Robert. When he realizes there has been an earthquake, he jumps up and informs Robert that he has to go check on Frankie. The narrative then takes us back to Grace and Frankie. Grace leans down under the table to check on Frankie, and Frankie says, "Massage my chest. It's a thing." Grace scoffs, "It's not a thing I would do." Just then Sol rushes in and immediately rattles off what is obviously the specific information Frankie needs. "It was a 4.3 lasting 6.8 seconds. No casualties, outages, or serious damage." Frankie is visibly relieved. Sol asks, "Are you belly breathing?" When she says, "no," he gets under the table with her to rub her chest and count her breaths. Once Frankie calms down and is willing to come out from under the table, Sol says, "I should go." Seeing that this makes Frankie sad, Sol asks, "You hungry…Maybe a bite?"

At the restaurant, Sol sends Robert a text message saying he's running late. Sol leans in and says to Frankie, "It feels good just to look at you." Heartbroken, Frankie frowns and says, "Don't do that. I'm not ready for that." Then she asks him why he kept his relationship with Robert a secret for so long. Sol replies, "It went from sex to love. If I told you…" Frankie interrupts, "You would have had ended our marriage." Sol says, "I still love you and our family," to which Frankie adds, "…and Robert."

Suddenly, there is an aftershock, and they both dive under the table. Rubbing Frankie's chest, Sol says, "I never thought we'd be doing this again." Frankie pushes his hand away from her chest as the waiter leans down and asks if they want

FIGURE 6.1 Grace offers Frankie anti-anxiety medication to calm her after an earthquake
Source: *Grace and Frankie* 2015.

FIGURE 6.2 Sol gets under the table with Frankie to rub her chest
Source: *Grace and Frankie* 2015.

the dessert menu. Without hesitating, Sol says, "We'll have the carrot cake and two forks, please." Out of habit, Frankie smiles and says, "Thank you" to the waiter as if they had done it a thousand times.

When Sol returns to the home he shares with Robert, Robert is jealous and upset. He says, "Why did we blow up our lives if you're going to go running back to your wife?" Sol appears shocked that Robert doesn't understand. "There was an earthquake!" Robert rolls his eyes with annoyance, something he shares with Grace, but he is no longer angry.

Grace and Robert also rely upon each other. Although they never loved or even liked each other as much as Frankie and Sol did, they shared a very traditional and heteronormative life and raised two children together. They too know each other well and are willing to have each other's back. Grace assists Robert in planning his wedding to Sol, and Robert reminds Grace of what makes her special and encourages her to date a much younger man. The four of them problem-solve when their children get in trouble, and all are present for the birth of Frankie's first grandchild.

Perhaps most important, Frankie and Grace have strong poly affective ties to each other. They do things for each other like providing reminders to take medications, emotional and financial support, and each encouragement to do everything from having orgasms to maintaining their independence and autonomy as they age. They even build a business together by designing and marketing a vibrator specifically for older women. Despite (because?) they do not have sexual desire for each other they are able to build poly affective bonds that are far more effective than dependent children, marital partners, or extended kin in securing their well-being.

FIGURE 6.3 Grace and Frankie, poly affective besties
Source: *Grace and Frankie* 2015.

As they all rely and depend on each other, they forge emotional, material, and psychological bonds, and it is in the doing of reliance and dependence that they build family ties. They have, in other words, a relationship that looks very much like media representations of heterosexual marriage in that their differences are always a source of humorous conflict (like many family comedies), but the bond is strong, enduring, and fulfilling. Significantly, these emergent poly affective familial bonds are not built from sexual desire or romantic love. In fact, it is the demise of their heteronormative marriages that opens narrative space for them to build something new: Something rather polyqueer. All four of the aging characters express and act upon strong sexual desire, but, significantly, desire and romance *for each other* are neither the basis for nor the defining feature of their connections. And yet, their post-heteronormative relationship network as four is narrated as the key to their individual happiness *and* their safety and security as they age.

The polyqueer content in *Grace and Frankie* opens up narrative space for an alternative narrative about the role the couple and heteronormative family must or should play as we age. The show suggests that poly affective relationships with other aging adults, including "exes," can fulfill the material, emotional, and psychological needs that heterosexual culture tells us are supposed to be filled by spouses, adult children, and extended kin. Although the show would not fall under Willey's (2016) rubric of dyke antimonogamy, it does offer something similar. It challenges the heteronormative and amatonormative assumptions that relationship successful is defined by marital or couple longevity where marriage and being a couple hinges on the presence of sexual desire, sharing a household, and subordinating all other relationships. *Grace and Frankie* is a narrative glimpse of how relationships can change over time for the better and of how security, health, and happiness can be found through, of all things, divorce, re-arranged living arrangements, and building poly affective ties with former spouses, their partners, and others. As a representation of familial ties that are not based on sexual desire and romance it provides a polyqueer alternative to the heteronormative family and kinship script. Importantly, the show *Grace and Frankie* is not *about* polyamory, but the narrative is antimonogamy, or as Willey (2016) suggests, "rather inspirational" and "suggests an ethic of destabilization." Though it is not a representation of dyke antimonogamy, it is, I would argue, a narrative of poly antimonogamy (more on this later). The show doesn't prescribe heteronormative relationships *or polyamory* as a remedy to the structural challenges and gender injustices that come with aging, and thus, it destabilizes heteronormative coupling and family ties as the only remedy for those challenges and injustices.

Cat Dancers: Poly ties, bisexual visibility, and interspecies kinship

The documentary film *Cat Dancers* (Fishman 2007) follows the careers of Ron and Joy Holiday and their assistant and life partner, Chuck Lizza. Together, they formed one of the first and most successful exotic big cat entertainment acts in the 1950s. The film features Ron Holiday in what appears to be an on-camera interview. He narrates his life with Joy, Chuck, and their big cats from the very beginning when Ron and Joy met in high school to the tragic end. The filmmaker weaves together Ron's narration with home movies of their life together. Ron is an instructor at Exotic World, an animal refuge that took the big cats when Ron lost Joy and Chuck, so in addition to the home movies and Ron's interview we see Ron instructing new employees at the refuge about the nature of big cats. During classroom instruction, Ron illustrates the unique relationship humans have with big cats by telling stories about his relationship with Joy and Chuck Lizza.

The film begins with Ron saying to the camera, "I know how it ended, but I'd rather have a beautiful dream." The dream, as narrated by the film, was polyqueer kinship with Joy and Chuck, and, as I will argue below, with the cats. Ron never explicitly states that he, Joy, and Chuck were polyamorous, but as the interview continues, we learn that they were all sexually involved, shared a romantic love as three, and lived together for 14 years.

Ron and Joy began their friendship in high school, and, until Joy went away to college and returned with a bombshell figure and a platinum blonde dye-job, Ron never considered her as a potential sexual or romantic partner. Ron says:

> I sat down with her and I said, "Look. We never had sex. You're like a sister to me always. Now I look at you completely different. You are absolutely gorgeous, and I think I'm in love with you." That night, god I was so drunk on wine, and we made love.

Later, Ron describes how, when Ron and Joy had their act in Las Vegas, Siegfried (of Siegfried and Roy) had a crush on Ron and would send flowers to his dressing room. Ron says with a hint of humor and catty disgust, "He wasn't my type. He was too femme."

Until Chuck arrives in the narrative, there is something un-self-consciously queer about the Holidays' relationship. Ron describes the time when he and Joy met Tennessee Williams. According to Ron, Williams had just encountered an adoring fan, and when the woman turned to go, Williams whispered to Ron and Joy, "Watch what she's going to say about me when I leave the room…Such a faggot! I'm sure he's going out to cruise the sailors." Then Ron says, "And that's when he became like a father to us. It was one of our first lessons to accept people for what they are."

Ron describes his and Joy's first encounter with Chuck Lizza. "Joy was the first person to lay eyes on Chuck. And she said, 'Ron. Wait til you see the surprise I have for you…He's to die for.' He was damn cute. He was a gorgeous male. And he was all man."

When Chuck came to the Holidays' ranch to assist them in training and performing with their cats, a poly relationship bloomed between the three of them. In the film, Ron describes it this way:

> It just happened one night. Joy was gone. And it happened. And when Joy came home I had this grin on my face and she read through me like that (snapping fingers). "I saw him first." That's what she said. And that's how we started. It was not…a rape. It was just something that happened that was beautiful. What happened after that is we became lovers. The three of us. Joy had encounters with him alone. Of course she did. But not the first time.

They were not publicly out about their polyamorous arrangement. Ron says, "Our life was very secret. We never showed affection back stage. Anywhere. No one knew really what Cat Dancers were." They each had separate bedrooms, but considered themselves married. They each wore a necklace with three entwined gold rings to signify their marriage to each other.

Despite not being "out" publicly about their poly relationship, sometimes they would coyly hint. For instance, in an interview with a newscaster, Joy said about their big cats, "We don't create people haters. We just get them really as young as you can. This way they're convinced we're Mom and Dad. Most cats… sometimes don't have one Dad. They have two Dads. One Mom and two Dads."

Ron wistfully describes how perfect life was for him during their 14-year poly relationship.

> I think the human race is archaic. They need labels, which is very, very sad. When Chuck came into our life, the intimacy we had spiritually, everything made us three of the most unique people. No one held anyone. And true love I think that's the only way it can work. There were no contracts to say I own

FIGURE 6.4 Joy tells a reporter that some cats have "two dads," while the proud "dads" look on
Source: *Cat Dancers* 2007.

you like what happens in many marriages. If someone wanted their space for a couple of days, they got their space for a couple of days.

Here Ron describes something that, quite explicitly, is a departure from heteronormative definitions of sexual identities and the labels, roles, and rules that heterosexual culture requires of marital relationships. He is attracted to Joy because she embodies a 1950s' version of feminine perfection (platinum blonde, curvy figure), and he desires Chuck because he was a "gorgeous male" and "all man." Without using the words "bisexual" or "polyamorous," Ron paints a rather queer desire for two people who embody the feminine and masculine extremes, and how the poly configuration of their relationship allowed him to have it all. He describes how blissfully happy he was to be in this polyqueer relationship with Joy and Chuck, "I don't think there is a human being in the world that could say he is as happy as I was. There was nothing that I wanted in the world. I had the most beautiful animals. I had the two most beautiful people in the world. A male and a female."

As rendered in the film, Ron's bisexuality is an emergent feature of the poly relationship he shares with Chuck and Joy. His seemingly unintelligible sexuality makes sense only after Chuck joins the act and Ron describes how perfect it was to have a manly man and gorgeous woman *at the same time*. In an analysis of representations of bisexual characters through poly relationships, Wayne Bryant (2004) concludes that filmmakers "simply do not understand polyamorous relationships"

(226). The reason is because, although the characters are presented as "genuine polyamorous bisexual characters," they are not embedded within stable poly family situations. "In almost all cases, the message that viewers receive is that poly relationships are unstable at best, and painful besides" (Bryant 2004: 226). This is not the case in the documentary *Cat Dancers* (Fishman 2007). Although the story is one of pain and loss (Ron no longer has a relationship with Joy and Chuck for reasons I won't go into here so as to not ruin the narrative trajectory of the story), the film does not portray the poly relationship as unstable or the source of pain and loss. Alexander and Anderlini-D'Onofrio (2012) write:

> [W]hen bisexuality is "real" (in a symbolic and a material sense), then the nature of love changes too. On the one hand, in a monosexually discursive context, the supreme act or moment of love is the perfect communion of two people. On the other hand, in a bisexually discursive context, this perfection, this supreme communion, cannot fulfill its potential unless it includes at least three participants. Hence, the bisexual "real" is a discursive context where the nature of love changes from an exclusive, dyadic system to an inclusive one that expands beyond the dual and into the multiple.
>
> *(17–18)*

In the film, the nature of love expands, not just to multiple adults, but also to the cats.

In the quote above from Ron, he said about his life: "There was nothing that I wanted in the world. I had the most beautiful animals. I had the two most beautiful people in the world." The "beautiful animals" are right there with Joy and Chuck in Ron's version of happiness. In fact, as narrated in the film, the big cats are an inextricable part of the polyqueer familial relationship between Ron, Joy, and Chuck. For instance, the archival footage of home life for Joy, Ron, and Chuck as they play with, discipline, and nurture the cats looks very much like pre-digital era home movies made by heteronormative families. I don't know if there was home footage of the humans interacting with each other without the cats present, but if there is, the filmmaker chose not to include it. Instead, the cats are central, and, given the interactions between them and their human parents, they are rendered as central to the family as human children are in home movies. This, combined with the news footage in which Joy says that the cats have one mommy and two daddies and Ron's interweaving of stories about his love for Joy and Chuck as he instructs students at the animal refuge about the nature of big cats, situate the cats as part of the family—as kin.

Although one might perceive the way Ron talks about the cats and their relationships with them as strange, I want to suggest that the "strangeness" stems from heteronormative ideas about sexual identities and a denial of (asexual) interspecies kinship bonds. As rendered in the film, the Holidays, Chuck Lizza, and their cats appear to be engaging in a kind of interspecies, polyqueer kinship. By weaving Ron's stories and the film footage together, the film stretches the definition of family and kinship so far beyond heteronormative prescriptions for genetic relatives that it snaps the genetic line completely. By narrating a familial connection between Ron, Chuck, and Joy and extending it horizontally to the big cats, kinship can include, not only multiple, non-related adults, but also *other species*. In an analysis of dog/human intimacies in literature, Alice Kuzniar (2016) writes,

> Dog love…has the potential of continuing and furthering the work of queer studies that interrogates the binaries that arise from inflexible gender and sexual identity categories. Our affective life with its fluctuating sensual needs, devotions and obsessions can be complex and inconsistent in ways that call into question self-definitions based primarily on sexual preference. Object choice as in the case of the pet can complicate, as does the fetish, a simplistic adherence to male-female or hetero-homosexual binaries when defining one's intimate self. In other words, to admit that one's object choice might not always be restricted to one's own species means to loosen the power granted sexual identity categories to socially regulate the individual.
>
> *(206–207)*

Kuzniar (2016) goes on to write:

> one of the major repercussions of pet love is that it reorients companionship and kinship away from the normative strictures of heterosexual coupling, and the traditional family. Taken seriously, it enjoins us to redefine bonds of privacy, succour, and habituation.
>
> *(207)*

Building on this idea, I would argue that queer kinship bonds might not always be restricted to one's own species. As inter-species, polyqueer narrative, *Cat Dancers* "loosen[s] the power granted sexual identity categories to socially regulate" (Kuzniar 2016: 207) with whom we foment kinship bonds.

Shortbus: Building polyqueer community through a-romantic sexual relationships

While *Grace and Frankie* offers representations of poly affective ties and *Cat Dancers* tells the story of interspecies, polyqueer kinship, the film *Shortbus* (Cameron Mitchell 2006) is a narrative about finding queer community through a-romantic, sexual relationships. A-romantic sexual relationships are ones in which people are sexually involved, care for each other, but romantic love is neither the impetus nor the goal of engaging in sexual relations. Because a-romanticism de-couples romantic love and sex, it challenges heteronormative imperatives to nest the two together. To the extent that heterosexual culture braids together sexual desire and romantic love as central to scripts for building family, kinship, and community, narratives of community built upon sex or sexual cultures that are not an expression of romantic love challenge heteronormativity even if the sex is between cisgender men and women (Berlant and Warner 1998).

The independent film, *Shortbus* opens with up-close, seemingly abstract shots of an object. Once the camera pans out, the Statue of Liberty emerges as the object. Panning out further, the camera travels over a vivid New York cityscape enhanced to look almost as if it is a colorful painting. As the camera zooms into a particular window in a particular apartment we meet James, a cisgender, white gay man in a relationship with Jamie, also white and cisgender.

In this first scene featuring James, he is alone, naked, and on his back. He flips his legs over his head and tries to reach his penis with his mouth, but he isn't erect so he can't reach it. Eventually he uses his hand to cum into his mouth, and as he does, he breaks down crying. A voyeur, also white and cisgender, watches through a telephoto lens from a different building. We eventually learn that James suffers from debilitating depression and cannot "let feeling get past [his] skin." He also refuses to be anally penetrated by anyone, including Jamie.

We then meet Sophia, a Chinese-Canadian couples' therapist who is married to Brad. Sophia is introduced through a montage of her and Brad in many different coital positions and in several rooms in their house. In a post-coital cuddle, Sophia thanks Brad and says, "That was incredible." She tells him that she feels sorry for people who don't have what they have, and then she proceeds to tell him about a client who fakes orgasms. She says, "Faking is a perfectly legitimate way to bide time."

Then Sevren enters the film. Sevren is a professional dominatrix who is troubled by not having close relationships with other people. During a scene in which she is flogging a young man, the john asks her if she is a top or bottom in real life. Sevren replies, "This is real life." When the john asks her if she ever wants to have children, she says, "I want to do it by myself, in the dark, like a worm."

James and Jamie meet Sophia when they seek couples' counseling because they are thinking about "opening" their relationship. As Jamie says to Sophia, "We've been together for five years, and let's face it, monogamy is for straight people." After an altercation between Jamie and Sophia during the session (she slaps him in the face), she confesses that she has never had an orgasm and that she is "pre-orgasmic." Jamie suggests that they can help her with that problem. They do so by inviting her to a sex club called Shortbus.

When Sophia arrives, she is overwhelmed by seeing so many people having sex in the same room and dodges into another space reserved for only femme, feminine, and woman-identified patrons called the "pussy palace." Sevren is in the room with the other femmes. Sophia explains that she cannot orgasm, and the others describe what orgasm feels like and offer advice. Without asking, Sevren takes a polaroid picture of Sophia. Once it develops, Sevren writes her phone number on the photo and hands it to Sophia. It is the beginning of a friendship between them that carries on outside the club.

When Sophia returns to the group play room, she watches a woman have an orgasm. As the woman passes Sophia, she makes eye contact and smiles. Sophia

FIGURE 6.5 In the pussy palace, Sophia confesses that she is "pre-orgasmic"
Source: *Shortbus* 2006.

compares the satisfied, calm look on the post-orgasmic woman's face with her own twisted and frowning face in the picture taken by Sevren. Later in the film, Sophia will have her first orgasm while having a threesome with the couple.

Jamie and James are also at Shortbus where they meet Ceth (pronounced, Seth). They invite him back to their apartment where, after many awkward moments, they have a threesome. Jamie is rimming Ceth while Ceth performs oral sex on

FIGURE 6.6 "Pre-orgasmic" Sophia finally has an orgasm while having a threesome with a heterosexual couple in Shortbus
Source: *Shortbus* 2006.

James, and James is playing with Jamie's penis. Ceth requests that Jamie say something into his ass. Jamie starts to mumble, and Ceth says, "Louder! Louder! Sing something." Jamie begins singing "The Star Spangled Banner" into Ceth's ass while Ceth uses James's penis as a faux microphone and sings along with him. After James ejaculates, they collapse together in laughter.

Though strangers at the beginning of the film, all of the characters who are either uninterested in or having problems with "straight sex," find each other and solutions to their problems in the queer, sexual culture of Shortbus. As described by the genderqueer proprietor, Justin Bond, the name Shortbus refers to "the short one. A salon for the gifted and challenged." The challenge, as narrated in the film, is getting one's needs met in a hetero- and mononormative world. There are some bumps (and humps) along the way, but the solution to their problems, as told in the film, is (poly) queer bonds fomented in Shortbus through communication, mutual support, and having sex with each other and with strangers in the club.

Certainly, *Shortbus* is about the healing powers of the erotic and sex. From a polyqueer perspective however, it is much more. Not only is the sex healing, it is also portrayed as the source and expression of *friendship bonds*. These a-romantic connections are established through sex with people other than regular partners, and it is through these friendship bonds that the characters experience their breakthroughs. The film thoroughly challenges the hetero, mono-, and amato-normative popular cultural narrative that says satisfaction, fulfillment, and mental health can be found only through romantic love with a committed partner. Moreover, by coupling the explicit (un-simulated) sexual content with signifiers of the nation (the Statue of Liberty, the Star Spangled Banner), the film also sutures a-romantic sexual bonds with citizenship, thereby queering notions of belonging. The characters, in other words, find connection and solidarity through a queer sexual culture (within the walls of Shortbus), not through national identity or heteronormative coupling, family, or kinship. Berlant and Warner (1998) state:

> By queer culture we mean a world-making project, where "world"…differs from community or group because it necessarily includes more people than can be identified, more spaces than can be mapped beyond a few reference points, modes of feeling that can be learned rather than experienced as a birthright. The queer world is a space of entrances, exits, unsystematized lines of acquaintance, projected horizons, typifying examples, alternate routes, blockages, incommensurate geographies.
>
> *(558, emphasis added)*

Few people who see the film would question whether or not *Shortbus* offers a narrative portrayal of queer world-making as it is defined by Berlant and Warner. By adopting a poly gaze, however, we can see that queer world-making, as told in the film, *hinges* on relationships that extend beyond the couple and on friendship networks that are sexual, a-romantic, and also caring and supportive. In other words, without the poly content, it is difficult to imagine how this film (or any film?) could render straight, couple relationships as 1) queer world-making, and 2) a path to queer belonging. In her critique of scientific research on "pair-bonding" through sexual relations, Angela Willey (2016) writes,

> The special status of coupling depends on distinguishing it not only from casual or uncoupled sex but also from friendship, comradeship, and situational solidarity. Breaking down barriers between these naturalized categories has the potential to radically reshape how we understand the importance of sex to human nature. It calls us to rethink the pervasive cultural privileging of sexual relationships over other types of connections. It begs that we rethink the relationship of "falling in love" and "getting attached" to sex.
>
> *(72)*

By not privileging the couple, *Shortbus* queers the relationship between "falling in love" and "getting attached to sex." In fact, the film turns this equation on its head. The characters do not become attached, fall in love, or pair-bond by having sex. Instead, they find solidarity and support by having unattached, polysexual friendships. By the end of the film, there is no indication or guarantee that the relationships will continue into the future, and it doesn't matter. The happy ending is a moment, not a relationship. It is a fleeting, orgasmic moment when queer culture, polyqueer friendships, and a sense of belonging come together in a glorious yet fleeting collective effervescence.

Conclusion

In *Beyond Monogamy* (Schippers 2016), I suggested that the Noel Coward play *Design for Living* is a polyqueer narrative. Building on the insightful work of Sam See (2004), I argued that poly relationships and kinship are not as rare in our collective imagination as the absence of the word "polyamory" might suggest. Stated another way, I suggested that there are many representations of poly sex and poly relationships that are not explicitly about, let alone named, *polyamory*.

In this chapter, I adopted the poly gaze to explore how the television show *Grace and Frankie* and the films *Cat Dancers* and *Shortbus* queer notions of family, challenge normative ideas about who constitutes "family," "kin," or "community," and open up narrative space for queer world-making and belonging through a-romantic, polysexual friendship.

Heteronormative culture is built upon a definition of family consisting of a given set of roles and affective ties limited to marriage and genetic kin. Polyamory as a "love style" and subculture increasingly solidifies a definition of "family" that is consistent with heteronormative family—poly families consist of a given set of roles and expectations, multiple adults that in which the presence or absence of sexual desire defines the roles, dependent children, and households established based on sexual desire and romantic love. On the other hand, to the extent that polyqueer configurations of affective ties reject the notion of monogamous coupling based on sexual desire and romantic love as the only or best way to form familial relationships, there certainly is potential for queer world-making by *doing* affective ties and mutual support and companionship in ways that are unintelligible according to heteronormative definitions of sexual identity, family, and kinship. The show and films I explored in this chapter offer narrative and visual representations of what that might look like. Of course, *Grace and Frankie* is not the only television show and *Cat Dancers* and *Shortbus* the only films that feature polyqueer representations of familial, kinship, and community ties. Perhaps, by adopting a poly gaze, other scholars and critics might search for and find others.

Notes

1 Many polyamorists refer to poly family formation as DIY. Polyamorous family formation means rejecting the monogamous couple script and opening the definition of family to include more than two adults. Until recently, there were no institutionalized paths or scripts for building polyamorous families and kinship. However, as polyamory gains acceptance through the hard, cultural work of polyamorists and their allies, a path is being cleared by establishing specific roles and norms for building healthy, fulfilling, and enduring polyamorous families. As I and others have argued, the plural structure of polyamory opens up interesting potentialities for living a queer life, but it does not always and automatically challenge heteronormativity.
2 Polynormativity refers to polyamorous relationships that are heteronormative in all ways except by including more than two adults.

References

Ahmed, Sara. 2010. *The Promise of Happiness*. Durham, NC: Duke.

Alexander, Jonathan and Serena Anderlini-D'Onofrio. 2012. "Bisexuality and Queer Theory: An Introduction." In Jonathon Alexander and Serena Anderlini-D'Onofrio (Eds), *Bisexuality and Queer Theory: Intersections, Connections, and Challenges*. New York: Routledge, 1–19.

Anapol, Deborah. 2010. *Polyamory in the 21st Century: Love and Intimacy with Multiple Partners*. New York: Rowman and Littlefield.

Berlant, Lauren and Michael Warner. 1998. "Sex in Public." *Critical Inquiry* 24(2): 547–566.

Brake, Elisabeth. 2012. *Minimizing Marriage: Marriage, Morality, and the Law*. New York: Oxford.

Bryant, Wayne. 2004. "Bi Film-Video World." *Journal of Bisexuality* 4(3–4): 219–226.

Cameron Mitchell, James. 2006. *Shortbus* [Film]. THINKFilm.

Coontz, Stephanie. 2005. *Marriage, A History: How Love Conquered Marriage*. New York: Penguin Books.

Fishman, Harris. 2007. *Cat Dancers* [Film]. HBO.

Halberstam, J. 2005. *In a Queer Time and Place: Transgender Bodies, Subcultural Lives*. New York: New York University Press.

Kipnis, Laura. 2003. *Against Love: A Polemic*. New York: Vintage.

Kuzniar, Alice. 2016. "'I Married My Dog': On Queer Canine Literature." In Noreen Giffney and Myra J. Hird (Eds), *Queering the Non/Human*. New York: Routledge.

Mint, Pepper. 2004. "The Power Dynamics of Cheating." *Journal of Bisexuality* 4(3/4): 55–76.

Rosa, Becky. 1994. "Anti-monogamy: A Radical Challenge to Heteronormativity." In Gabriele Griffin (Ed), *Stirring It: Challenges for Feminism*. New York: Taylor & Francis, 107–120.

Schippers, Mimi. 2016. *Beyond Monogamy: Polyamory and The Future of Polyqueer Sexualities*. New York: New York University Press.

See, Sam. 2004. "Other Kitchen Sinks, Other Drawing Rooms: Radical Designs for Living in Pre-1968 British Drama." *Journal of Bisexuality* 4(3–4): 29–54.

Sheff, Elisabeth. 2014. *The Polyamorist Next Door: Inside Multiple-Partner Relationships and Families*. New York: Rowman and Littlefield.

Willey, Angela. 2016. *Undoing Monogamy: The Politics of Science and the Possibilities of Biology*. Durham, NC: Duke University Press.

7

CONCLUSION: FROM POLY READING TO POLY LIVING

Poly lives in a time of neo-fascism

My goal in this book was to present the poly gaze as a lens through which anyone, regardless of their relationship status or experiences, can read texts against mononormativity. I suggested that the poly gaze is useful for identifying poly resonances from the past and present and for reading mononormative narratives from a poly rather than mono perspective. I have focused on film, television, journalism, historical biography, and social science research on campus hookup cultures. As I have merely scratched the surface of how the poly gaze might be utilized, my hope is that others pick up where I left off. For instance, others could mine for poly resonances in other kinds of media like music, theatre, literature, dance, and social media (to name a few) and sociologically analyze the workings of mononormativity and poly narrative.

The specific texts that I analyzed are merely a small sampling of where we might place the poly gaze. For instance, I focused specifically on how journalists narrate FLDS polygamy. Left unanswered, of course, is how journalists narrate poly lives in other contexts. Similarly, I offered a poly analysis of research on campus hookup cultures. Given the ubiquity of mononormativity, it is highly likely that other social science research is littered with mononormative assumptions about the social world. Others, I hope, will adopt a poly gaze to begin critically engaging those literatures. I have no doubt that the historical biographies I've discussed here are not the only ones that describe people living poly lives in the past or present. Not only can we adopt a poly gaze to parse how biographers have written these lives; more important, perhaps, historical biographers could adopt a poly gaze to search for and find poly resonances where we might not expect them. In other words, there is, no doubt, a treasure-trove of poly resonances in all kinds of research and media and many people who have lived or are living poly lives but have not been acknowledged or, if they have, are described in mononormative ways. My hope is that this book is a small nudge toward finding those resonances.

Another goal of this book was to begin identifying poly resonances in unexpected places. In 2015, at the first International Conference on Contemporary Intimacies and Non-Monogamies, Daniel Cardoso called for building a poly archive. Although Cardoso's focus was on archiving poly activism, I hope that this book encourages others to include historical figures who have lived poly lives and media representations of poly resonances. This, I suggested in Chapter 4, is important for challenging mononormative histories of intimate and political life and for interrogating collective understanding of what it means to live a good life. Because I am defining poly as encompassing but not reducible to contemporary polyamory, I have tried to begin archiving something more akin to poly resonances rather than polyamorous people or media that feature polyamory. Obviously the films *Savages* and *Splendor* would be included in a poly archive, but so must *Grace & Frankie, Cat Dancers*, and *Short Bus*. The poly resonances in these media texts open up poly to include affiliations of mutual responsibility and care in addition to sexual non-monogamy or romantic love.

As I have argued in this book, the poly gaze does not end with uncovering poly resonances and lives or revealing mononormativity in the stories we tell about intimate relationships. As a sociological lens, it is equally concerned with what these stories articulate about how happiness is achieved and who is deserving of a good life. As we search for poly resonances, it is not enough to be pleasurably hailed by positive representations of polyamory; we must also pay close attention to what poly-positive narratives say about how to live a good poly life and about who is deserving of happy poly endings.

While consuming media that feature or portray poly lives can be deeply pleasurable and provide some semblance of feeling "normal" in a mononormative world, we must resist the pull to normalcy. We have learned from critiques of homonormativity that spinning tales about the normalcy of polyamory inevitably reproduces sexual and relationship hierarchies as a legitimate rationale for deciding how resources, authority, and deservedness are distributed. In his book, *Feeling Normal: Sexuality and Media Criticism in the Digital Age*, F. Hollis Griffen (2016) acknowledges that consuming media representations of LGBTQ characters and themes can feel "normal" for LGBTQ audiences. Though feeling normal can be deeply pleasurable and lead to a sense of belonging, we must be aware of how representations of LGBTQ lives often fold potentially political content into neo-liberal and homonormative ideas about what constitutes a "good life." Griffen writes:

> The desire for social legibility is a compelling one, which most sexual minorities—most people, even—understand as being necessary if one is to have a livable life. As such, this book takes seriously the desires presented in gay and lesbian movies, television programs, and online media—not to rescue them or condemn them, or even to argue that they are more progressive or regressive than they seem at first glance. Rather, the book considers gay and lesbian media evidence of the thorny terrain of politics in the twenty-first century,

where ideas about sexual minorities are animated through narratives about individual happiness, and political claims get refracted through vague assertions related to personal transcendence. In gay and lesbian media, sexual politics present narrative problems that are solved by individual triumphs, which most frequently occur by amassing financial wealth or finding romantic love.

(Griffen 2016: 2)

Although a person living a poly life might feel "normal" and derive a sense of pleasure and belonging by watching the films *Savages* and *Splendor*, the poly gaze encourages us to examine those feelings as complicit in reproducing deeply problematic attachments to class, ethnicity, nation, and the heteronormative family.

In Chapter 6, I suggested that poly lives are not necessarily about sexual partnerships, marriage, or relationship longevity. Instead, the texts I analyzed offered a narrative glimpse of how poly connections can be represented as temporary, trans-species, and built upon mutual responsibility and caring and not necessarily on marriage or romantic love. Although none of the texts I analyzed in Chapter 6 offer representations of poly normalcy, they do open up the imagination to how poly resonances and connections can challenge our desire to feel normal. I would like to suggest that a desire for acceptance through normalization, especially in the contemporary context of Trump America and the rise of neofascism in the United States and Europe, takes us down a path of assimilation rather than transformation.

As polyamory emerges in the popular consciousness as an intelligible and viable relationship style, narratives about polyamory are too often grounded in neo-liberal assumptions about choice, free will, and consumption (Rambukkana 2016), and reproduce colonial narratives about "natural" human sexuality, and sexual exceptionalism (Willey 2016). Relationships are presented as a set of options on the menu or different styles one might pick from the rack. I have shown in Chapter 2 in my discussion of television portrayals of "suburban polygamy" that polygamists who live heteronormative, metronormative, and consumerist lives are portrayed in mainstream media as worthy of acceptance, if not rapt attention, because they are perceived as relatively "normal" compared with rural, religious, and isolationist polygamists. Absent from these juxtapositions is a sociological understanding of how representations of "good" and "bad" FLDS polygamists reproduce neo-liberal notions of good citizenship. Similarly, in Chapter 5 I argued against pursuing acceptance by telling stories about polyamory as exceptionally sexy, progressive, and enlightened. Depictions of polyamorists as white, middle-class, conventionally attractive, young, and heterosexual and representations of polyamory as more enlightened or fulfilling than monogamy, situate "acceptable polyamory" as the path to happiness and a good life. This simply replaces "good" monogamy with "good" polyamory. Not only does this gloss the variability in how poly relationships take shape and how they affect people's lives, it implicitly endorses the idea that heteronormative family life is a legitimate measure of being a "good

American." Whether it is monogamous marriage or heteronormative polyamory, in both cases citizenship and morality hinge on relationship status. People who are not in a monogamous marriage or a heteronormative, polyamorous relationship are implicitly or explicitly cast out of good citizenship. Furthermore, poly-normative representations limit what can be imagined as a poly life by presenting a specific kind of polyamory as "good" and, more important, they erase the political and social potential of poly sensibilities beyond the romantic and sexual.

This, I believe, is one of the most important aspects of the poly gaze. Searching for, analyzing, and archiving poly resonances beyond the romantic and sexual might reveal alternative ways of living a good life, but also a political life. In an essay about the intimate life of Alexander Berkman (Emma Goldman's life-long partner, Sasha, see Chapter 4), anarchist theorist, Jenny Alexander (2011) writes,

> I propose that it is now time to return, within Western queer, anarcho-queer and anarchist political and scholarly contexts, to considerations of intimacy. I am not advocating anything like a simplistic return to the lesbian continuum. Rather, I am concerned with all (consensual) non-blood-kin passionate inti-macies between people, historically and contemporaneously, which do not fit into categories defined by sex acts …Why should emotionally significant deep attachments where those concerned choose not share bodily fluids be deemed less socially significant than fluid-bonded states?
>
> *(39)*

I believe that if we limit what "counts" as poly representation to sexual non-monogamy or romantic polyamory, we will miss the potential to "see" what poly resonances *do* to notions of belonging, security, and mutual care and responsibility.

As discussed in Chapter 6, in her reading of the comic *Dykes to Watch Out For*, Angela Willey (2016) argues that dyke anti-monogamy is a model for fomenting ties that are not based on monogamous marriage or genetic ancestry. She writes:

> From ex-tended families to intergenerational friendships to cohousing (not to mention pets!), the world of DTWOF is a world of proliferating intimate networks founded on friendship and commitment to imagined community… By offering us a world in which each connection is but one model and but one relationship in the lives of each of these characters, and where sex is consequently decentered, this ethics offers instruments for invention…If knowledge and desire, the textual and the corporeal, are always enmeshed, this antimonogamy ethics, it would seem, has the potential to reorient our desires. And those queer feminist political desires, feminist science studies would suggest, have the potential to reorient our knowledges.
>
> *(Willey 2016: 119)*

Here I want to highlight how Willey links ways of relating to ways of knowing. Re-orienting our desires according to what she calls anti-monogamy ethics has potential to transform not just our relationships, but our ways of seeing and knowing the world. In other words, a poly gaze (as I've developed it here), when combined with an ethic of caring and mutual responsibility on the one hand and a political orientation toward social justice and change on the other, can perhaps become a lens for living as well as reading.

If we do so, poly living (in the way I'm defining it here) just might open up transformative paths that take us toward new models for fomenting alliances and connections and resisting the politics of hate and division that, within the United States and Europe, currently is presenting itself as the path to belonging. In an essay published on the *Los Angeles Review of Books* website, Jordy Rosenberg (2018) connects the dots between the rise of fascism in the United States and Europe and the disintegration of the nuclear family under the pressures of austerity. Neo-fascists, Rosenberg avers, are not interested in taking the moral high ground by championing the nuclear family. The current President of the United States is no paragon of heteronormative family virtue, and is, in Rosenberg's words, a "parody of the American presidential family romance." Instead, neo-fascists use the very real material insecurities experienced by citizens (and families) as a moment to resignify the sources of danger as external to the family (queers) and to the nation (immigrants).

> In a moment at which cultural politics has risen to its own obscene heights—not just a veil for the outright murderous intent of so many present policies, but truly a direct dog whistle to the fascists—it ought to come as no surprise that the specific surplus available for resignification is the excessive affect gluing itself to the figure of the family (as a figure for the nation more broadly).
>
> *(Rosenberg 2018)*

Contemporary neo-fascism, Rosenberg argues, "has a strange, parasitic relationship to the energies of the family's *decomposition*... Edifices are shattering, and who knows what new subjectivities and social formations will come of it." In this chaos around the definition and viability of family, Rosenberg (2018) calls on queers to step up to fill this cultural vacuum.

> What will become of us? I don't know, but I'm saying that fascism tries to usurp everything, including or especially unruliness, and I'm sorry, but no: the supernova of the family's destruction ought to be ours to redefine... This—the family, and all its contortions—is a certain kind of hell, no doubt—and, to recall the issue with which I began—a ground that we must not surrender. We queers know the contours of this particular hell so well; we know how to inhale its phantasmagoria air, and—if we are committed to a radical politics that does not seek assimilation so much as transformation—we know how to exhale elements of a different composition.

In an analysis of the influence of Ayn Rand on contemporary culture and politics, Lisa Duggan (2019) also suggests that contemporary U.S. culture is in transition.

> We are in the midst of a major global, political, economic, social, and cultural transition—but we don't yet know which way we're headed. The incoherence of the Trump administration is symptomatic of the confusion as politicians and business elites jockey with the Breitbart alt-right forces while conservative Christians pull strings. The unifying threads are meanness and greed.
>
> *(xiii)*

In this book, I have argued (and I hope demonstrated) that the stories we tell about monogamy, polyamory, and poly connections can be ones of either assimilation or transformation. I also suggested in Chapter 6 that narratives about poly relationships outside of the rubrics of love, sex, and romance and across species offer a glimpse of transformations in intimacy, belonging, and kinship. For the remainder of this chapter, I would like to shift from the poly gaze as a method for reading texts to the poly gaze as a way to live in the world. How might thinking poly rather than mono help us imagine forms of belonging, kinship, and politics that refuse assimilation and embrace transformation?

Heteronormative notions of family and kinship are linear and hierarchical, and lines of kinship and belonging hinge upon shared ancestry and marriage. Monogamous marriage joins two and only two familial lines, and notions of kinship stretch to former and future generations and are constrained and limited by blood and marriage. Monogamous marriage then, establishes boundaries and borders around those who are defined as kin and those who are not. Sarah Ahmed writes:

> What needs closer examination is how heterosexuality becomes a script that binds the familial with the global: the coupling of man and woman becomes a kind of "birthing", a giving birth not only to new life, but to ways of living that are already recognisable as forms of civilisation. It is this narrative of coupling as a condition for the reproduction of life, culture and value that explains the slide in racist narratives between the fear of strangers and [145] immigrants (xenophobia), the fear of queers (homophobia) and the fear of miscegenation (as well as other illegitimate couplings).
>
> *(Ahmed 2015: 144–145)*

In other words, monogamous coupling reproduces and supports dynamics of racial, national, or ethnic borders.

Poly ways of relating, in contrast, replace hierarchical structures of "family" bounded by marriage and blood with horizontal expansions of kinship and belonging based on care and mutual responsibility. Kinship built upon poly rather than mono attachments extends notions of mutual responsibility to non-blood, non-marital others. Rather than fomenting ties that bind, poly connections are ties that expand and produce a sense of responsibility in multiple and sometimes unexpected directions. For instance, Angela Willey (2016) points to how lesbians have been fomenting anti-monogamous relationships all along as an alternative to the heteronormative nuclear family *and* heteronormative, sexual and romantic polyamory. Describing the poly community of which she was a part, Serena Anderlini (2008) writes:

> Their belief systems are flexible and in flux yet deliberately out of alignment with the mainstream. They share an expansive sense of love and sexual expression that involves consensual sharing of emotional and erotic resour-ces...If savage capitalism produces the criminalization of love and the self-destructive cultural practices that ensue, this expansive sense of love is the antidote to that poison, the disease that is the cure.
>
> *(144)*

Anderlini (2008) goes on to write:

> They form multipartner relationships that multiply the emotional resources available to the group and enable players to share more agreeably. They engage in a variety of amorous and erotic practices that enable players to share pleasures more inclusively. They resolve conflicts via nonviolent communica-tion that involves honesty and personal intimacy. They tend to be good par-ents because their amorous practices generate an abundance of social energy for parenting in their communities.
>
> *(133)*

While Anderlini paints quite a glowing if not utopian picture of polyamory's potential, she and Willey tap into the rhyzomic structure of poly affiliations as a contrast to horizontal family formations grounded in monogamous marriage.

As I discussed throughout the book, family and nation go hand-in-hand to define good citizenship. The notion of family and nation hinges upon and reproduces borders and barriers as the very definition of belonging. Poly lives encourage us to reject barriers to affiliation and connection and to open up our sense of belonging to include others who, at first glance, might not seem to be part of the "family" or the "nation." If blood and marriage are no longer the affective tie that binds us in the context of poly relationships, might a poly sen-sibility open us up to an alternative sense of belonging that is grounded in neither family nor nation?

I do not mean to say that forming polyamorous relationships is the remedy for the politics of hate and division that now plague much of the global north. Instead, I wonder if looking at the world with a poly rather than a mono sensibility might open up conceptual space to envision a way to be together and work toward change—a sense of togetherness that doesn't hinge on sameness or difference but instead is established through mutual responsibility to each other, our communities, other species, and the world while acknowledging difference. Again, taking her cue from Alexander Berkman, Jenny Alexander (2011) writes:

> But so, perhaps even more urgently at this juncture in the West, does the re-remembrance and revaluation of intimacies without definitive sexual aims or definitions passionate friendships, affectionate touch between those who are neither family nor lovers, acts divorced from erotic conclusions. These traces in history are not simply embryonic forms of queer sex before gay liberation (although to strategically read them as such has had political value). They are part of the complexity and the potential of net-worked human interactions. Not grounded in fucking but in feeling, such intimacies cross the boundary between straight and queer.
>
> *(36)*

A poly approach to living, then, is not about having polyamorous relationships with more than one romantic or sexual partner. Poly living would mean defining mutual responsibility and care horizontally rather than vertically and to be open to unpredictable but mutually beneficial alliances and connections. In their book, *Multitude*, Hardt and Negri (2005) describe network political organizing in remarkably poly ways.

> To a certain extent these postmodern, post-Fordist movements complete and solidify the polycentric tendency of earlier guerrilla models. According the classic Cuban formulation of *foquismo* or *guevarismo* the guerrilla forces are polycentric, composed of numerous relatively independent focus, but that plurality must eventually be reduced to a unity and the guerrilla forces must become an army. Network organization, by contrast is based on the *continuing* plurality of its elements and its network of communication in such a way that the reduction to a centralized and unified command structure is impossible. The polycentric form of the guerrilla model thus evolves into a network form in which there is no center, only an irreducible plurality of nodes in communication with each other.
>
> *(83, italics in the original)*

There is no center. Relationships potentially extend outward in ever changing and unpredictable directions, and connections are fomented through a plurality of nodes in communication with each other. Poly sensibilities provide a model for forming affective ties beyond the nuclear family, and, as discussed in Chapter 3, as an alternative to the impersonal, cold, and sometimes exploitative world of campus hookup cultures. If we jettison romance and sex as *the criteria* for defining relationships, we can perhaps envision poly ties that do not hinge on the presence of sexual desire or romantic feelings, but instead on all kinds of commitments to each other. In the introduction to an anthology on anarchy and sexuality, Jamie

Heckert and Richard Cleminson ask, "Can an ethic of care in practices of mutual aid create unexpected solidarities?" (Heckert and Cleminson 2011: 10). That is, might poly ties (not bounded by marriage and ancestry, but also by romance and sex) offer a transformative way to not only build kinship, but also build political solidarities?

Finally, I want to suggest that a poly approach to fomenting connections and solidarities, whether intimate or political, offers something to strive for that does not throw the intimacy and mutual interdependence baby out with the hetero-normative, neo-liberal, mean-spirited bathwater. Instead of rejecting caring, con-necting, and taking responsibility for each other, perhaps we could adopt horizontal, rhyzomic, and queer notions of belonging. We might seek what Ahmed (2015) calls queer affect, something that emerges by inhabiting norms differently.

> We can posit the effects of "not fitting" as a form of queer discomfort, but a discomfort which is generative, rather than simply constraining or negative. To feel uncomfortable is precisely to be affected by that which persists in the shaping of bodies and lives. Discomfort is hence not about assimilation or resistance, *but about inhabiting norms differently.* The inhabitance is generative or productive insofar as it does not end with the failure of norms to be secured, but with possibilities of living that do not "follow" those norms through. Queer is not, then, about transcendence or freedom from the (hetero)norma-tive. Queer feelings are "affected" by the repetition of the scripts that they fail to reproduce, and this "affect" is also a sign of what queer can do, of how it can work by *working on* the (hetero)normative.
>
> *(155)*

What can living and thinking poly do to how we inhabit (hetero)norms around belonging and caring for others? In conversation with Michael Hardt about the relationship between love and politics, Lauren Berlant says,

> When you're asking for social change, you want to be able to say there will be some kind of cushion when we take the leap. What love does as a seduction for this is, and has done historically for political theory, is to try to imagine some continuity in the affective level. One that isn't experienced at the his-torical, social or everyday level, but that still provides a kind of referential anchor, affectively and as a political project.
>
> *(Davis and Sarlin 2011)*

Might poly connections built upon care and mutual responsibility (regardless of whether or not we like, love, or fuck each other) offer a bridge between the love and happiness we're all encouraged to seek in conventional, romantic or sexual relationships on the one hand and some other, transformative kind of belonging on the other? Could a poly affect have a relational *and* political valence? In times when us-against-them borders are drawn through white supremacist, heteronormative, and nationalist logics, we need to reconfigure notions of belonging and alliance. At the risk of sounding poly-anna-ish, I wonder if poly affect as a political valence might open up new ways of imagining transformative ways of connecting with each other—ways that are grounded in mutual responsibility and care rather than sexual love and romantic notions of family and marriage. Perhaps we have much more to learn from Audre Lorde and Emma Goldman after all.

References

Ahmed, Sarah. 2015. *The Cultural Politics of Emotion*, 2nd edn. Edinburgh: Edinburgh University Press.

Alexander, Jenny. 2011. "Alexander Berkman: Sexual Dissidence in the First Wave of Anarchist Movement and Its Subsequent Narratives." In Jamie Heckert and Richard Cleminson (Eds), *Anarchism & Sexuality: Ethics, Relationships and Power*. London: Routledge, 25–44.

Anderlini, Serena. 2008. *Gaia and the New Politics of Love: Notes for a Poly Planet*. Berkeley, CA: North Atlantic Books.

Davis, Heather and Paige Sarlin. 2011. "No One is Sovereign in Love: A Conversation between Lauren Berlant and Michael Hardt." NOMOREPOTLUCKS. Online journal accessed March 1, 2019. http://nomorepotlucks.org/site/no-one-is-sovereign-in-love-a-conversation-between-lauren-berlant-and-michael-hardt/.

Duggan, Lisa. 2019. *Mean Girl: Ayn Rand and the Culture of Greed*. Berkeley: University of California Press.

Griffen, Hollis. 2016. *Feeling Normal: Sexuality and Criticism in the Digital Age*. Bloomington: Indiana University Press.

Hardt, Michael and Antonio Negri. 2005. *Multitude: War and Democracy in the Age of Empire*. New York: Penguin Books.

Heckert, Jamie and Richard Cleminson. 2011. "Ethics, Relationships and Power: An Introduction." In Jamie Heckert and Richard Cleminson (Eds), *Anarchism & Sexuality: Ethics, Relationships and Power*. London: Routledge, 1–22.

Rambukkana, Nathan. 2016. *Fraught Intimacies: Non-Monogamy in the Public Sphere*. Vancouver: University of British Columbia Press.

Rosenberg, Jordy. 2018. "The Daddy Dialectic." *Los Angeles Review of Books* (online magazine), March 11. https://lareviewofbooks.org/article/the-daddy-dialectic/#!.

Willey, Angela. 2016. *Undoing Monogamy: The Politics of Science and the Possibilities of Biology*. Durham, NC: Duke University Press.

REFERENCES

Evans, Caroline and Lorraine Gamman. 1995. "The Gaze Revisited, or Reviewing Queer Viewing." In Paul Burston and Colin Richardson (Eds), *A Queer Romance: Lesbians, Gay Men and Popular Culture*. London: Routledge.

Logan, Joshua. 1967. *Camelot* [Film]. USA: Warner Brothers/Seven Arts.

Munoz, Jose Esteban. 2000. *Disidentifications: Queers of Color and the Performance of Politics*. Minneapolis: University of Minnesota Press.

Schippers, Mimi. 2002. *Rockin Out of the Box: Gender Maneuvering in Alternative Hard Rock*. New Brunswick: Rutgers University Press.

Schippers, Mimi. 2016. *Beyond Monogamy: Polyamory and the Future of Polyqueer Sexualities*. New York: New York University Press.

INDEX